Everyday Teacher Leadership

Everyday Teacher Leadership

Taking Action Where You Are

Michelle Collay

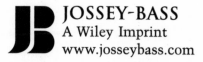
JOSSEY-BASS
A Wiley Imprint
www.josseybass.com

Published by Jossey-Bass
A Wiley Imprint
989 Market Street, San Francisco, CA 94103-1741—www.josseybass.com

Library of Congress Cataloging-in-Publication Data

Collay, Michelle.
    Everyday Teacher Leadership : Taking Action Where You Are / Michelle Collay.
        p. cm
    Includes bibliographical references and index.
    ISBN 978-0-470-64829-2 (pbk.); ISBN 978-1-118-02307-5 (ebk);
    ISBN 978-1-118-02309-9 (ebk); ISBN 978-1-118-02308-2 (ebk)
        1. Educational leadership. 2. Teacher participation in administration. 3. Teachers—
    In-service training. I. Title.
    LB2806.C527   2011
    371.1'06—dc22

                                                                            2010049620

Printed in the United States of America
FIRST EDITION
PB Printing   10 9 8 7 6 5 4 3 2 1

Contents

About the Author

Michelle Collay is professor in the Department of Educational Leadership at CSU East Bay, Hayward, California. A former public school music teacher, she is a scholar-practitioner who integrates teaching and scholarship in higher education and PK–12 settings. Her research interests include teacher professional socialization with attention to how life experience shapes teachers' professional identities. Collay coaches school leaders engaged in professional learning communities, constructivist teaching and leading, and equity-focused inquiry. Her previous books include *Constructivist Learning Design* with George Gagnon and *Learning Circles: Creating Conditions for Teacher Professional Development* with Diane Dunlap, Walter Enloe, and George Gagnon. Collay has also authored many articles on the topics of leadership, equity, and urban education. She stays grounded as a parent leader in her children's schools.

Acknowledgments

The voices in this text represent urban teacher leaders who have dedicated their lives to teaching and leading others. Their reflections are profound, honest, and heartfelt. They have tilled the soil, planted the seeds, and enabled the growth of students, peers, and all educational leaders who share their journey. I extend my deepest appreciation to these colleagues who have been my teachers.

I thank my mentors for encouraging me to follow this path when the way wasn't always clear. Linda Lambert, Rob Proudfoot, Diane Dunlap, Joanne Cooper, Liz Wing, Sandy Gehrig, Barbara Storms, and others are teachers and leaders who guide my footsteps as I continue to ask, "How did you learn to lead?"

I have been supported in my writing by my colleague and friend Peg Winkelman and my thinking partner and husband, George Gagnon. George is also a colleague in this work and helps me focus on what matters. Kate Gagnon at Jossey-Bass helped craft an authentic framework so the leadership of my teacher colleagues could inform the field in powerful ways.

Finally, I acknowledge my two school-age children, Von and Nina, for providing so much material for my thinking about teaching. Ultimately, parents and teachers share the work of educating young people, leading them outward to become leaders in their own right.

Everyday Teacher Leadership

Introduction

> Good teaching cannot be reduced to technique;
> good teaching comes from the identity and integrity
> of the teacher.
>
> —*Parker Palmer*

Parker Palmer's words open this section and this book because his emphasis on the identity and integrity of teachers resonates deeply with me. I embrace the term "good teaching" rather than "good teacher," because the former represents work we strive to do every day. The latter implies judgment of individuals rather than the work itself, perhaps by each teacher of herself or one teacher of another. Teachers are judged as good or bad by each other, students, parents, administrators, policymakers, and media. Much of the research on the characteristics of a "good" teacher or an "excellent" teacher is divisive, lending credence to the idea than some have what it takes and others don't. We're all good teachers some of the time, but we strive to do good teaching all of the time. I acknowledge that there are some teachers who should not be in classrooms, but for the purpose of this work, I take the stance that most teachers strive to teach with integrity every day.

Teaching with integrity requires leadership. Teaching is leading; teachers are leaders. This book focuses on how teachers already lead and how they can learn to lead more purposefully. Some teachers have a more developed professional identity and are more effective instructors, colleagues, and leaders. Mature teachers may lead with greater skill, but they don't *become* leaders at some point in the future. They already lead. As my professor remarked after he heard me say I was *learning* to play the bassoon, "No, you're *playing* the bassoon. Someday you'll play it better!"

Teachers construct a professional identity long before they enter their own classrooms and develop that identity further as they establish, refine, and extend their practice. Teaching practice is inherently an act of leadership. Most experienced teachers manifest a fully formed teaching identity, whereas early years' teachers exhibit less confidence. I can tell when I'm fully inhabiting my role as teacher and when I'm not. Most teachers can tell you whether their colleagues are professionals—that is, fully embracing the work of teaching with integrity. When I observed student teachers day in and day out, I used the phrase "your teacher self" to characterize that sensibility. We know it when we see it and when we don't, but it's very hard to describe. Good teaching mediates the process of identifying, disrupting, and creating or reestablishing more equitable outcomes for students. Great teachers do this all the time; good teachers strive to do it and succeed most of the time. Disrupting inequity from within the system is hard work, and few of us feel successful all the time or even most of the time.

Teaching Is Leading

Teachers come into the classroom from many cultural backgrounds and with a variety of professional experiences. Many are drawn by a deeply human desire to serve their communities, to engage in work that is meaningful, to "make a difference." Entry into the daily work of classroom teaching is no mean feat, requiring courage, persistence, and leadership from the earliest days. The intersection between learning to teach and leading is reviewed by Cherubini in an examination of young teachers' identity development: "It was clear from this research that participants struggled to negotiate the paradox of loving the idea of being a teacher, but not necessarily liking the work as teacher. Of utmost interest to this research, however, was the outcome that despite the uncertainties of their responses to the professional and emotional challenges of teaching, beginning teachers exercised dimensions of leadership. Their impetus was to impact positively upon the students entrusted to their care."[1]

My colleagues and I make the case throughout the chapters of this book that teachers lead by working directly with students and others who influence student learning inside and beyond the classroom. Teachers act on behalf of students by planning instruction, creating curriculum, collaborating with colleagues, taking initiative, taking the lead, and co-constructing practice on numerous levels. As reported earlier in this section, even the newest teachers understand their work as leadership, and in the following example those actions are characterized as "leadershipping," according to Cherubini:

> Beginning teachers, at various times and under varied circumstances, described how they exercised their influence in the classroom and school community in informal roles as a *lead* teacher, as a *leader* of initiatives, and as serving in a *leadership* capacity (representing the leadershipping concept as noun, verb, and adjective). Participants often took the *lead* to express their perspectives in discussions with their mentors. They were willing to take the *lead* by inviting students to celebrate their cultural differences. Participants perceived themselves as valuable *lead* persons in facilitating networking opportunities with other new teachers to share their approaches to differentiated instruction and long-term planning. Indicative of others, these participants adamantly suggested, "We do know what we are doing," and "It's not about just taking ideas and not giving back." Last, participants reported a heightened awareness as the school year progressed of students' unique learning styles and, as a result, assumed *lead* roles by collaborating to design specifically adapted lessons with other faculty.[2]

The young teachers in Cherubini's study offer us a powerful reminder that the newest members of our profession lead by advocating for students, taking the path of owning expertise, developing professional relationships, and reaching beyond their classrooms to ensure students were served. When we reflect on our earliest days of leading the learning of others, we can see evidence of leadership.

My Own Journey

My own journey as an educational leader began over thirty years ago, when I was encouraged by my former high school band director to accompany five busloads of sixth graders and their teachers for a week of outdoor education. At nineteen, I wasn't much older than the campers, but I was expected to make a contribution and do my part to encourage learning. Five summers of residential summer camp leadership in roles ranging from horse wrangler and cabin counselor to program director nurtured the seeds of teaching as a career for me. I attended three colleges for three degrees and took lots of courses about teaching, but it was my camp counseling experience that fundamentally influenced my beliefs about teaching and learning. Camp was designed by Irv Newman, an old-school progressive educator. It was a place for seven- to fourteen-year-olds to move through a developmental process from structured days to choice making about activities to self-organized days. The trappings of everyday material life were minimized, and children learned to learn. An essential ingredient of camp was mentorship between the director and staff, staff and campers, and among campers. Irv hired a variety of counselor personalities so that "every camper would have at least one adult they could relate to."

Formal training as a music major provided another critical part of my teacher training. Teaching and learning in the fine arts is different from other disciplines in some ways—the ways that stand out for me now include the discipline of daily practice, a well-understood apprenticeship, growing responsibility as a tutor and mentor, performance alone and with others, and integration of mental, physical, and emotional development. After struggling through high school and "not learning,"[3] I found an intellectual challenge I could meet and a like-minded community of practice to join. My music teachers had a profound influence on my identity as a learner, and I wanted to join their ranks.

I entered my first classroom as a certified teacher at twenty-six. As the youngest member of a junior high school staff, I studied teaching and learning in the public school setting and began to ask questions about the profession of teaching. A life-long interest developed about this question in particular: How are individuals socialized into a community of practice? And the counterpart of that question: How do individuals influence their community? My early observations made it clear that we each come to the classroom with different values and purposes, have different expectations of ourselves, our students, and our colleagues, and strive, sometimes without success, to reconcile our beliefs with the beliefs of others. We don't agree about the big ideas of education. Those differences play out every day in every way, shaping and molding our professional identities.

Why did my colleagues have such different beliefs about teaching and learning? What was the source of those different beliefs? Their classroom practices and the philosophies that guided those practices ranged from behaviorist to progressive. Some believed every child could learn and was deserving of an education, while others demonstrated a painful lack of faith in young people. Several senior teachers became mentors and advocates, reaching out to a struggling youngster with advice, modeling, moral support, and good humor. Priscilla came into my math class and gave me suggestions about organizing my lessons, June advised me to send my most difficult student to her room on those days I couldn't keep her in her chair, and Wayne invited me to sit in with his band on Tuesday nights so I could learn the basics of directing a jazz ensemble. In contrast, the art teacher told me I was a sucker to join the school-based management team, and the most senior English teacher banished me from the staff room after I naively advocated for a student she had suspended for insolent behavior.

Early years in my own classroom were followed by many more years of classroom visits as a mentor of first-year teachers, student-teacher supervisor, and school coach. I have worked in the most rural schools of North Dakota and the most urban schools in Oakland, California. Throughout that time, I was also a member of several university faculties, where I was an instructor of undergraduates and graduate students, teachers, principals, and central office leaders. I learned that the same patterns of engagement, membership, and leadership prevailed in those university departments. Some of my colleagues were able and willing to socialize me into the work of university teaching and learning, while a few had become cynical and distant from the community. Different individuals took responsibility for different aspects of the work, each bringing a different set of skills, beliefs, and practices. With few exceptions, my current colleagues teach with integrity and dedicate themselves to the service of students and to the profession. Our perceptions about membership and leadership vary, but in every case "good teaching" is a perennial quest to understand the nature of learning and the social construction of knowledge. I now understand that good teaching is itself an act of leadership.

I believe teachers are leaders from the first moment we engage in learning with another. We teach long before we enter our first certified position, and we carry beliefs about learning and leading into the classroom and the school. The act of choosing "school teaching" is itself an act of leadership. I have always questioned acceptance of a hierarchical "ladder" of professional responsibility in schools. In a relatively flat organization with students at the center of the enterprise, most teachers need resources and support, not a supervisor. On one hand, schools are complex extensions of the government, built on religious and community foundations, and teachers are representatives of the government. On the other hand, schools reflect the social networks of smaller neighborhoods and communities, containing the best and worst of human nature. Teachers are so much more than purveyors of the government's education policies and mediators of intellectual content. We are scholars, practitioners, generalists, specialists, facilitators, mediators, and moderators. We are parents, siblings, and children, members of religious groups, atheists, and activists. We are all these things and more. Teachers are leaders.

We are sometimes gardeners who have accepted a plot of land to care for when we didn't choose the seeds. Within our classrooms, we recognize the gifts and challenges our students bring, and we nurture those seeds into more fully developed plants. We till the soil, water the seedlings, and struggle to resist pulling the weeds. We strive to see the space as a garden filled with plants of which we don't yet know the names. The ground may lack certain nutrients or the right conditions for all the plants that come up, but our task is to keep all of them alive, not just those that are best adapted to the conditions.

Other times we are mechanics, often without the right tools to repair the systems in which we and our students live and work. We tinker with the machinery while knowing the machine is not designed to do the job. We borrow tools from our neighbors to make the short-term repair in hopes the machine can continue to function, even as we recognize its limitations. We walk away from this broken machine in frustration, only to return the next day because that's the only machine we have. There are few other forms of education for most working-class and poor students. We educators have chosen to work with all students, taking responsibility to do our best with the materials and resources we have. Accepting this role is an act of leadership.

The Purpose of This Book

This book has three purposes: the first is to explore the assumptions that inform our thinking about teaching as an act of leadership. We who work in education have internalized beliefs about what leading is, who can lead, and how teachers are or are not leading. Working in classrooms with children and young people is leadership, and differentiating leadership by separating "teaching" from "teacher-leadership" from "leaders" reinforces hierarchical roles. I assert that educational leadership begins in the classroom and extends to all domains of teaching and learning, including grade-level teams, departments, schools, districts, and communities. Teachers lead by taking actions that improve the conditions of learning for others.

The second purpose of this book is to present the voices of teachers about teaching as leading. We stand to learn much more about leadership from teachers who believe schools are for student learning. My school-based colleagues are teachers in every socioeconomic situation and geographic region who lead in classrooms, schools, and beyond. The voices in this book represent a particularly urban experience, yet their learning is instructive for all who believe every student deserves an education. Throughout these chapters, teacher leaders from some of the most challenging urban schools in the nation share their thinking about leading for equity by advocating for students. Teachers seeking socially just learning for students embrace their calling as educational leaders and compel colleagues, parents, and faculty to think differently about teaching as leading. They have been my teachers. Together we strive to reconceptualize the unfortunate distinction that has made "teacher" a qualifier of "leader." Their voices, stories, and passion extend and broaden the meaning of leadership.

The third purpose of this book is to offer ideas, structured opportunities, and processes for leadership exploration—about what we already do as leaders, about how our life experiences inform our leadership, about the various dimensions of school leadership, and about expanded notions of educational leadership. These applications are designed to support "critical reflection"[4] in the tradition of transformative learning. At the end of each chapter, I synthesize the key ideas or considerations and suggest resources that might be useful.

This book is for anyone with an opinion about the role of leaders in transforming education. This book is for those who question the effectiveness of formal leaders in schools and for those who think they are not leaders. This book is for those who have already internalized their "leader self" and are fully enacting leadership from every corner of the school. And this book is for anyone who believes embracing teaching as leading will help sustain his or her own professional growth and improve the educational experiences of students, families, colleagues, and the community.

How This Book Is Organized

This book integrates my thinking about leadership as informed by educational leaders who have been my students and colleagues over the past thirty years. Each chapter begins with an examination of how teachers come into the work of teaching as leading. I include big ideas from relevant research, but draw primarily from the experiences of teachers. I share the stories of teachers who have studied leadership in our program by excerpting essential ideas from their written reflections about leadership actions in schools. These colleagues are full-time teachers who were pursuing a graduate degree in educational leadership. There are additional resources that may be useful to those conducting professional development or designing coursework. At the end of each chapter, I include processes that invite introspection about leading in schools. The inquiry activities can be used by individuals or teams and can be modified or recombined in any way that is useful.

The book is divided into six chapters that explore various perspectives on and levels of school leadership. Each chapter has an introductory section to set the context, a main section portraying the experiences of educational leaders, and a final section with applied activities. The order of the chapters follows the life-work journey of most teachers—after starting with a brief history of school leadership, the chapters then address how teachers are socialized into the profession, why teaching is leading, and describe ways teachers enact classroom-based leadership through systems-changing leadership. The chapters follow the leadership of teachers from the first formal work setting of the classroom outward, but they can be read separately as needed.

In Chapter One, I offer a brief review of how North American schools came to have managers, along with the emergence of the teacher as staff to be managed. During the long journey from home- and church-based schooling to our current industrial and corporate models, teaching and management diverged and managers got the title of "leader." Teachers continue to lead from the classroom outward, and effective principals share and support that practice, but the term *leader* was assigned to those outside the classroom. Questioning the convention of principals as managers and teachers as staff is essential to the premise of the book—we have internalized these assumptions about what leadership is and who can lead, and these assumptions restrict our understanding about how teachers already lead.

In Chapter Two, I explore the individual roots of educational leadership, beginning with the influence of teachers' life histories on practice. We choose teaching—or it chooses us—because of our own experiences as children and young people. Those experiences compel us to carry back the water; that is, to carry on traditions of advocacy and service that supported us as students and to disrupt and change practices that were discriminatory. Our own teachers, mentors, and family members influence our values as we step into our own classrooms for the first time. We then join a community of practice that includes the roles of instructor, parent, sponsor, and political advocate.

As we "learn to teach," we are already teaching. Every dimension of our personal lives informs leadership.

In Chapter Three, I focus on the core of school leadership—the everyday teaching and learning of adults and students. Engaging students in learning content is complex and requires a sophisticated approach to curriculum, meaning "to run the course." Co-construction of knowledge is much more than "covering" the topic, teaching as telling, or professing. For students to learn, teachers, parents, and community members must join them and run the course together. With time, practice, and experience, many realize that instructional practice is one of the most powerful forms of educational leadership. Teachers come into education to teach students, and their integrity as school leaders reflects that commitment. Teaching is leadership.

In Chapter Four, I consider the kinds of leadership that emerge when teachers advocate for their students within and beyond the classroom. Initial planning for student learning may begin there, but it quickly becomes evident that systemic factors beyond the classroom influence what teachers can do with and for students. Teachers identify external forces that support or hinder their ability to create a productive learning environment for students. By accepting the role of student advocate, teachers strive to mitigate the worst effects of poor policy and to strengthen useful policy. Collaboration is leadership.

In Chapter Five, I offer a leadership approach used with teacher leaders in our leadership program that supports school transformation. The Equity Plan was developed by a faculty team to be a transformative pedagogy for site-based leaders. The material is drawn from leaders' experiences and takes their colleagues through a process of identifying inequitable policies or practices at their school, engaging them in addressing the problem, and enacting change at the site. The cycle of inquiry or action research is led by teachers. Inquiry is leadership.

Finally, in Chapter Six, I review ways teachers have worked in partnerships within and across communities to effect sustainable change. The kinds of transformation needed in schools may be centered in the classroom, where teachers are the most powerfully positioned to lead that change. The most effective teachers, however, connect with various types of networks to infuse additional strands of learning into the classroom setting and to support their own professional development. Policymakers and school reformers must recognize the power of these networks to support teachers and their students from the ground up, rather than promoting ineffective, top-down mandates that do not reach students. Teachers lead through establishing and maintaining partnerships.

How to Use This Book

This book can be used by individuals, small groups, or staffs. It can be used as a course textbook in leadership programs. The chapter material can be read and discussed to set up the inquiries, or the inquiry guidelines can provide a starting point for individuals or small groups. The chapters are designed to build on each other, but they can also be used individually. Constructing knowledge is best done in the company of others, but collaboratives are not always available. Read about the main ideas, listen to the voices of our colleagues who lead work in schools, and examine your own thinking about the considerations or takeaways at the end of each chapter.

Use this book as a text: faculty members teaching courses about leadership more generally or teacher leadership specifically will find this book helpful as a course or program text. I have used the inquiries in the chapters with practicing teachers in university- and school-based settings. Any inquiry can and should be modified to serve teachers and their students. The end user can make decisions about which inquiries to use and which settings to use them in.

Use this book in schools and in professional development settings. Any text or guide is most useful when used with relevant topics in the context of real work to be done.

Using Systematic Inquiry

The excerpts presented in this text were documented within a cycle of systematic, professional reflection over a two-year period during which educational leaders met on a weekly basis. Teachers engaged in a series of facilitated oral reflections and written processes that supported leadership development. Conversations were conducted in pairs, small teams, and with the whole group. Readings, applied activities, and colleagues' daily experiences provided the text for the work. Participants wrote about their goals, successes, challenges, and actions as part of their study. All the participants were based in schools, and most worked in small teams at their sites, generally with other individuals who were not enrolled in any formal program.

The inquiries associated with each chapter were designed as part of a teacher leadership development program. Inquiry—"to seek truth, information, or knowledge; examination of facts and principles"—is a broad concept, and in this case the scope of inquiry can be as simple as reflecting on a prompt or as complex as leading a research project at a district. I have facilitated similar inquiries in schools with grade-level teams, departments, and whole-school professional development. Professional reflection activities or inquiries used in this text are an iterative process of reflection and action.[5] Systematic, professional reflection includes storytelling, journal writing, description, reading others' work, interpretation, analysis, and action. *Critical reflection*[6] deepens the already vital process of storytelling or narrative by linking individual experiences to larger social patterns. Individual reflection opens the mind and heart, but collective reflection illuminates interdependence with others and connections to our work. Cycles of inquiry include taking action and reflecting again on those actions and outcomes. Developing a community of practice requires professional reflection and action with others and can be built into any professional development calendar.

Collaboration structures allow systematic professional reflection, but they do not ensure the development of an authentic learning community or community of practice. The power of collaboration resides in the commitment to a common purpose. Examples of powerful collaborative structures are offered in many resources including work on learning circles,[7] professional learning communities,[8] and communities of practice.[9]

The inquiries can be used in any order, but the sequence of chapters serves as a helpful guide here: teachers develop identities as leaders of others' learning before they enter the classroom. Once formally employed, teachers lead by engaging children and young people within their classrooms. Creating successful learning environments demands that teachers reach across classrooms and departments, then to colleagues throughout their schools. Finally, teachers reach out to district, agency, and nonprofit settings to more fully develop their craft in larger communities of practice. Leading the work of educating begins within us before we enter our own classroom and extends far beyond that classroom every day. The core of teaching is leading, and the scope of that leadership unfolds over time, place, and setting.

By offering a series of applied activities, I invite individuals, small groups, or seminar members to interrogate their thinking about teaching as leading, analyze their work as leaders, and evaluate how they lead in their school or other educational settings. Throughout the text, the scope of leadership actions is described and reconsidered through the lens of teaching as leading. At the end of each chapter are applied activities that can be used by individuals, teams, or larger groups. On the web site are examples of completed activities. Use them in any way that is useful for thinking more deeply about professional identity development and working toward transformative school leadership.

Everyday Teacher Leadership

This book is about teaching as leading and how teachers lead in schools every day.

Everyday is defined in Merriam-Webster's dictionary as "encountered or used routinely or typically; ordinary." The irony of this definition is what compelled me to write this book. While teaching has not been perceived as "leadership" in our society, and acts of leadership by teachers occur every day in sometimes routine ways, such leadership is hardly ordinary. Rather, leadership embedded in teaching is extraordinary. The first definition of *extraordinary*—"going beyond what is usual, regular, or customary"—is educative in this discussion. "Going beyond" captures how we think about leadership generally and, I suggest, about good teaching. The second definition of extraordinary— "exceptional to a very marked extent"—is not entirely apt here either, as everyday teacher leadership is not exceptional, but common. The final definition offers food for thought: "employed for or sent on a special function or service." Teachers on a quest to advocate for students or colleagues may be pressed into special functions or services, to be sure.

Over the course of this book, my colleagues present examples of good teaching as the most powerful form of educational leadership. I will also hold the concept of "good teaching" as what those of us who strive for excellence do. I challenge all of us to rethink our long-held beliefs that what *teachers* do and what *leaders* do are different acts. Throughout the chapters of this book, I invite you to consider and reconsider your beliefs about the profession of teaching and the ways teachers lead, from the ordinary to the extraordinary, from the commonplace to the exceptional. Teachers lead every day by taking action where they are.

Notes

The epigraph to this chapter is drawn from P. Palmer, *The Courage to Teach: Exploring the Inner Landscape of a Teacher's Life* (San Francisco: Jossey-Bass, 1998).

1. L. Cherubini, "A Grounded Theory Analysis of Beginning Teachers' Experiences: Illuminating Leadership Capacities," *International Journal of Teacher Leadership* 1(1) (2008): 27. http://www.csupomona.edu/ijtl.

2. Cherubini, "Beginning Teachers' Experiences," 27.
3. H. Kohl, *"I Won't Learn from You" and Other Thoughts on Creative Maladjustment* (New York: New Press Books, 1995).
4. S. Brookfield, *Becoming a Critically Reflective Teacher* (San Francisco: Jossey-Bass, 1995); K. Brown, "Leadership for Social Justice and Equity: Weaving a Transformative Framework and Pedagogy," *Educational Administration Quarterly* 40(1) (2004): 79–110; P. Cranton, *Developing Adult Educators: Using Transformative Learning and Critical Reflection to Improve Practice* (San Francisco: Jossey-Bass, 1996); J. Mezirow, "On Critical Reflection," *Adult Education Quarterly* 48(3) (1998): 185–198.
5. D. Schön, *The Reflective Practitioner: How Professionals Think in Action* (London: Temple Smith, 1983).
6. K. Brown, "Leadership for Social Justice and Equity: Evaluating a Transformative Framework and Andragogy," *Educational Administration Quarterly* 42(5) (2006): 700–745.
7. M. Collay, D. Dunlap, W. Enloe, and G. Gagnon, *Learning Circles: Creating Conditions for Teacher Professional Development* (Thousand Oaks, Calif.: Corwin Press).
8. R. Barth, *Learning by Heart* (San Francisco: Jossey-Bass, 2004); K. Bielaczyc and A. Collins, "Learning Communities in Classrooms: A Reconceptualization of Educational Practice," in *Instructional Design Theories and Models, Vol. 2,* ed. C. M. Reigeluth (Mahwah, N.J.: Lawrence Erlbaum Associates, 1999); R. DuFour and R. Eaker, *Professional Learning Communities at Work: Best Practices for Enhancing Student Achievement* (Bloomington, Ind.: Solution Tree, 1998); S. Hord, *Professional Learning Communities: Communities of Continuous Inquiry and Improvement.* (Austin, Tex.: Southwest Educational Development Laboratory, 1997).
9. E. Wenger, *Communities of Practice: Learning, Meaning, and Identity* (Cambridge, U.K.: Cambridge University Press, 1998).

1

A VERY BRIEF HISTORY OF SCHOOL LEADERSHIP

> History cannot give us a program for the future, but
> it can give us a fuller understanding of ourselves,
> and of our common humanity, so that we can better
> face the future.
>
> —*Robert Penn Warren*

Volumes have been written about the history of North American schooling, and it is certainly beyond the scope of this book to revisit our history in any depth. I provide a brief sketch here of how school management has evolved over the past 150 years, intending to offer a fuller understanding of teachers who lead. I consider historical and cultural influences on educational roles in schools, rather than defining what teacher leadership is and who teachers are as educational leaders. The organization we call *school* was created in response to culture-specific ideas about how formal education should be structured. Most, if not all, of these concepts have been challenged and revised over time, yet the very foundation of nineteenth-century European Judeo-Christian values lies firmly beneath our feet. Those structures and organizing features have been rendered invisible over time and, like dusty worn rugs, need a good airing, if not disposal. Like many other observers, I believe modern schools were never designed for learning and their potential to serve modern society grows more limited by the day. Meanwhile, teachers lead the work of educating young people and each other in schools. I hope the briefest sketch will illuminate some unexamined premises of teaching as leading and allow us to better face the future.

Leading Learning Past and Present

The physical organization of contemporary schools in North America may seem timeless to those who are second-generation or higher North Americans, yet the model is only one hundred and some years old. "Modern" schools' emergence parallels the twentieth century's evolution from more rural to more urban—from family-centered businesses and cottage industries to industrialization. Skilled work done by both genders was learned through apprenticeship with a craftsperson. Literacy development for European-Americans in the eighteenth and nineteenth centuries typically occurred through religious education for both genders, and formal academic study was reserved for the middle class. Whether individuals were immigrants or members of established communities, reading and ciphering were learned in homes and churches. Schooling in the early United States reflected attempts to establish common schools in the Thirteen Colonies, but individual communities held tightly to cultural and religious values and their right to inculcate their children with those values. New York City fathers established "free schools" in the early 1800s, seeking to provide basic education and moral values to children from homes where parents were uneducated (and presumed to be immoral). In the largest urban areas, tenement-dwelling children attended factory-like warehouse schools. In rural communities both North and South, one-room schoolhouses represented another path to formal schooling. In both cases, only rudimentary study was the norm. Until the mid-twentieth century, only middle- and upper-class children received a formal education that could prepare them for university admission. Working-class youth trained in the trades—which required formal but often nonliterate apprenticeships—or in unskilled jobs that required little or no formal training. "College prep" coursework was then, as it is now, reserved for the privileged class.

"Educational leadership" in homes, religious settings, and one-room schoolhouses was provided by parents, clergy, teachers of both genders, and other community members. Teaching throughout the nineteenth century was a transient occupation in which young men might hold a position as teacher for a few years before moving on to other lines of work. After the mid-1800s, young women followed the same pattern. They taught younger children in short stints, usually until they became established with their own homes and families. In Southern black communities during Reconstruction, small, formerly clandestine schools continued to serve freedmen, both adults and children. Teachers were not professionals and did not organize themselves in large settings. Notions of the "principal teacher" followed the need to organize or manage many teachers under one roof and were established mainly in large, urban schools.

Organizational structures of the largest Northern schools reflected industrial practices established in the nineteenth century, thus creating the school structures we know today. In this structure one principal (with or without assistants) manages many teachers, and that principal is charged to carry out the dictates of governments that finance the school. Suburban and the few remaining rural schools followed the lead of the largest schools, emulating graded classrooms, subject-centered scheduling, emphasis on start- and end-times, bells, and the need to stay at one's desk for the duration of instruction. Such standardization was seen as a natural by-product of modernization. Large, factory-like schools were designed to prepare the masses with vocational training to work in similar settings when they came of age, not to prepare members of a democratic society. Therefore, schools needed managers, not instructional leaders.

Different Leaders for Different Schools

Throughout the twentieth century, some educational leaders challenged the industrial model of schooling, but their ranks were small. The schools they established were often idiosyncratic and elite, barely touching the masses in production-line schools. Examples of progressive education that repudiated industrial model schools include John Dewey's lab school at the University of Chicago, the Waldorf School, Froebel's kindergartens, and schools based on Adler's Paideia philosophy or Maria Montessori's methods. In the latter half of the twentieth century, the Coalition of Essential Schools, a network of progressive educators and parents, continued the traditions of developing critical thinking, collaborative, project-based learning, and community partnerships. These few schools were only available to families of privilege, however, and their individualized, constructivist, and student-centered approaches to teaching and learning have had little influence on the greater schooling enterprise.[1] The purpose of Progressive schooling was to create an educated citizenry that could fully participate in the democratic process. This foundational understanding runs counter to the capitalism-based belief that schooling is preparation for factory work. Progressive schools were often established and led by charismatic leaders who had strong beliefs about school as a place to develop the human mind and spirit. To quote Montessori, "The greatest sign of success for a teacher . . . is to be able to say, 'The children are now working as if I did not exist.'" Societal beliefs that youngsters should be self-directed learners remain controversial, even as most citizens agree that industrial-era schooling is not adequate to modern societal demands.

Schools Reflect Society

After World War II, more children were attending the growing numbers of schools, but they were still in racially segregated classrooms. As the era of race-based civil rights took root in the mid-1950s, schools became more than a reflection of the multifaceted society in which they sat. Race- and gender-based discrimination was challenged in the courts, and schools became the locus of systematic attempts to integrate communities. Because of civil rights case law, schooling for all was established as a legal right, not a privilege. The stated goal in federal policy was equal education for all, and schools became the primary container in which societal inequities might be measured and rectified.

One outcome of court-ordered school racial integration was an acknowledgement that even though laws permitting schools to be "separate but equal" had been overturned, American schooling continued to reflect and perpetuate social and economic disparities. Most school systems were theoretically desegregated through edict and policy, but in reality remained separate and unequal. Large urban schools continued to serve low-income and immigrant newcomers, while white working-class families with some mobility moved to the suburbs. Affluent families continued to enroll their children in private schools. Public school leaders' management tasks now included formal requirements to educate all students, whether majority or minority, regardless of race, gender, or disability. Educators in public schools are therefore now required to lead broader societal reforms, whatever their roles and responsibilities, however large or small the institution. Educational leaders face the same dilemmas prevalent in the larger society: role, experience, race, gender, class, sexuality—our own as well as those of our constituents—dictate opportunity and shape the educational process.

A small but persistent progressive movement continued throughout the second half of the twentieth century and into the new century. In the 1970s, progressive educators established "schools within schools," such as academies, magnets, and other approaches to individualizing education. These more personalized approaches are evident in contemporary reform efforts—for example, the creation of smaller schools within large high schools and theme-based schools led by community partnerships. While John Dewey's efforts to disrupt the worst practices of systematic, routinized factory schooling failed on a large scale, these progressive glimpses into more humane and culturally responsive learning environments offer hope to many underserved communities. These schools are also incubators for innovative leadership structures.

The Evolution of Leading and Managing in Schools

Leadership of formal schooling evolved throughout the twentieth century, reflecting societal changes and evolving perspectives on the purposes of schooling.[2] Activities associated with leadership moved from the province of individual teachers working with small groups of students to formal management of small, medium, and large organizations. The "leader" of the school was the principal-manager, and teachers, however formally educated or experienced, reported to that principal. When schools grew large and required management, the issues were primarily facilities, budget, staffing, and students. A retired principal told me his job in a rural elementary school required him to "Keep the boiler lighted and chase the dogs off the playground!" In Alaska, where he lived, keeping the boiler lighted was a serious matter. In rural schools, the superintendent might also drive the bus, coach the football team, and teach social studies. In large urban schools, formal leadership is usually distributed across a management team, in which the principal works with one or more assistants to manage the facilities, budget, staffing, discipline, and student mental and physical health.

Who Becomes a Principal?

For most of the twentieth century, school leaders were male and white, with a few exceptions. Women headed some small rural schools and some urban schools in the early part of the century. Southern African American communities were segregated from white communities, and the leaders of African American schools were black, as were the ministers of African American congregations and others in the professional classes. After laws were passed in the 1960s that rendered formal desegregation illegal, black principals were often displaced by white men, although the school staff and students remained largely segregated. Women's removal from and re-entrance into the principalship paralleled their engagement in the workforce in other fields before and after World War II. Ironically, in a "women's profession" such as teaching, the number of women principals does not yet reflect the gender ratio of the teaching workforce. The evolution of schools into larger consolidated centers actually reduced the number of women principals from a higher number in the 1920s to lower numbers later in the century.

School leadership patterns reflect race, gender, and class status in the larger society. Consider the following: in 2007–2008, the majority of public school teachers were women (about 84 percent at elementary schools, 59 percent at secondary schools), but only 59 percent of elementary principals and 29 percent of secondary principals were women. Demographic data from NCES for 2008–2009 indicate that 84 percent of principals were white, 10 percent were African American, 4.5 percent were Hispanic, 0.4 percent were Asian, and 0.6 percent were American Indian.[3] All things being equal, the ranks of principals should reflect teacher demographics, if not student demographics.

Certainly, greater societal influences on professional access and selection of majority and minority individuals for any role prevail in schools as well. Our "semiprofession" has long debated whether teachers are born or made, and there is a parallel debate about whether leaders are born or made. Most of us agree that while teachers and principals are required to have a credential, preparation is a minimum requirement. All professionals strive to move beyond basic preparation to good practice, so if teachers can develop their craft, the same should be true for administrators. Yet so-called "trait theory" pervades our thinking about leadership. Traits associated with effective leaders have included personal characteristics and temperament as well as managerial skills. Numerous studies do not support leaders having specific traits, but beliefs about the traits of a good leader persist. Those with the greatest social status in the larger society also have status in schools. The notion of the "hero-principal"[4] is alive and well at all levels of the educational enterprise. This image departs from the earlier "principal-teacher," as they were called at one time, who could do every job in the building, secure resources, and maintain a complex schedule for her teachers and herself. Current examples of the school leader as hero are evident in mission statements of nonprofit enterprises such as New Leaders for New Schools, Leadership Academies, and other like enterprises. Millions of dollars are invested into recruitment and training of the "best and brightest" corporate-style leaders as our profession struggles to pull the largest districts into the twenty-first century. New leaders are trained in corporate-style management, and teachers are seen as one of the resources to be managed.

Who Becomes a Teacher?

Teaching is considered a "semiprofession," and teachers are unionized workers for the most part.[5] While the management-staff metaphor is problematic for those who consider themselves full professionals, the concept of principal as boss is alive and well in contract language and in our collective understanding of how schools are organized and staffed. Whether one accepts my proposition that working directly with children is an act of leadership,[6] most people generally see the principal as "in charge" of the school and teachers as subordinates. This belief runs deep and is not easily disrupted by the many examples of teacher autonomy[7] and teacher leadership we observe in schools every day. The tangled roots of management and staff relationships have made "teacher leadership" a separate enterprise from school leadership. Teachers' perceptions of their autonomy and authority are shaped and reshaped by the organizational apparatus of school and the history of the profession.

Teachers strive to act in professional ways amid very con-flicting work cultures. Some research suggests that conventional leadership is "antithetical" to teachers behaving professionally.[8] Conventional leadership requires conventional followership, and the trappings of leading and following limit professional action. Teachers work in settings that demand sophisticated responses to complex problems, yet are expected to do what they're told or be labeled resistant to reform efforts. Conflicting expectations lead some to challenge the authoritative relation-ship between themselves and principals,[9] while others acquiesce or play along in what Hargreaves[10] calls "contrived collegiality." Even those models that sound more democratic come under fire by those who study reform. One example is the rhetoric of "dis-tributed leadership," a catchall term that implies more people have authority to make decisions.

Little research supports the efficacy of this approach[11] and, like many recommendations that emerge from studies of school leadership, the principal is charged to do the distributing. Teachers are *allowed* to have authority over their work, *chosen* for tasks, or *given* responsibility. In each case, teachers are sub-jected to, not agents of, leadership. No wonder some succumb to the condescension and withdraw or leave the profession altogether. It's understandable that when teachers are treated like line workers, some respond in kind and walk out the door at three o'clock. Many teachers work long hours after students leave, and some are admonished for breaking contract agree-ments. Union policy sometimes "protects" teachers' rights by forbidding them to convene in professional conversation beyond contract hours.

Most teachers transcend the constraints of conventional management-staff limitations, refusing to be deskilled by man-dated, scripted curricula, retaining their dignity in the face of labor actions, and keeping a professional countenance with all comers: students, parents, clipboard-wielding staffers, compli-ance officers, and errant journalists. Teachers lead in myriad ways from the moment they accept the job, whether they choose or are chosen to become formal leaders at a later time. Teacher race, gender, and class status influence how they experience authority,[12] but all teachers must enact leadership from their position in the social hierarchy.

Challenging the Dichotomy Between Site Leaders and Teachers

Studies of what traits make a good principal reflect what teachers, parents, and the general public think makes a person a "leader." Effective teachers display the same traits, but are they essential to powerful leadership for teaching and learning? These traits are seldom interrogated, but accepted as innate to effective leaders and include qualities like decisiveness, good management, and organization. The expectation that principals should also be knowledgeable about learning was less common in earlier decades, but the climate of accountability has heightened the need for principals to be "instructional leaders." Few principals, however, spend much of their time working directly with teachers and students. Most pertinent to this discussion, leadership "traits" often reflect historical patterns of race, ethnicity, gender, language, and other areas of perceived difference. The cultural and systematic exclusion of minorities from full membership as teachers and formal leaders reflects societal assumptions about who leaders are, rather than what they do.[13]

Through the last years of the twentieth century and a decade into the twenty-first century, little has changed in the organization and management of schools. Schools are not the great equalizer, but rather effectively reflect and reproduce inequities present in the larger society. Educators strive to close the widening opportunity gap between those who can squeeze into an outdated schooling model and the majority of the school-aged population that mainstream education excludes. Efforts to reach the poorest-performing students are stymied by social circumstance, outdated pedagogy, and the dearth of resources. Visionary educators in the least resourced communities struggle to establish and sustain charter schools or other forms of smaller, more intimate schooling environments and continue to fail the urban communities that they seek to serve. A generation of school reform efforts has not solved the century-old problems of schooling the least among us.[14]

Schools are touted as foundational to creating and sustaining a democratic society, yet schools continue to reproduce the most egregious of discriminatory patterns evident in the larger society. School leaders in a variety of roles are unwittingly complicit in replicating societal structures that sort, track, and limit access to an adequate and equitable education. The organizational and physical structures of schooling reflect deeply held nationalistic values of capitalism, competition, and prosperity. Unexamined, these embedded assumptions continue to shape schooling in very insidious ways, and conventional school leadership practices follow these assumptions.

In 1983, the National Commission on Excellence in Education published "A Nation at Risk: The Imperative for Educational Reform."[15] This report focused on the dire academic performance of public schooling in the United States compared with international counterparts. The findings and recommendations emphasized "content" learning and teacher quality, indicating that unless major reforms occurred and higher standards were set, American students would continue to fall behind. This call to arms echoed the post-Sputnik crises of the late 1950s, when the Russians beat the Americans into space and schools were charged to "catch up" with the Russians. The need for qualified teachers to address worsening student performance figures prominently in this report and subsequent reports. Every president since that time has implemented a version of national reform and recommendations, currently reflected in President Obama's Race to the Top. Each policy development demands more accountability by school leadership, unfortunately accompanied by less autonomy and efficacy to resolve the concerns every teacher already has.

Over the past thirty years, the pressures on educators to use content standards and raise test scores have created new twists and turns along the path of school leadership. On one hand, teachers have lost some of the professional gains made during the 1970s and 1980s, when progressive methods and teacher professionalism were gaining momentum. On the other hand, teachers are now more formally educated, and more of them obtain advanced degrees than thirty years ago. Contemporary teachers study leadership and reform, develop expertise in specific areas, and provide much of the formal leadership in schools. Positional leaders may be forced to decentralize authority because so much of the responsibility of raising test scores falls on teachers. Whether authority is distributed by the principal, wrested away from the central office, or emerges from a desire to make learning accessible to students, teachers have authority and are authorities in their own classrooms and beyond.

Teaching as Leading

Given the history of schooling and its less-than-adequate work conditions and job status, choosing to become a teacher at all is an act of leadership. Many new teachers undergo a professional hazing when they change sides of the desk, including starting their careers in economically challenged communities, starting weeks or months into the academic year as a long-term substitute or unplanned hire, managing multiple preparations, being assigned high numbers of lower-performing students, and being pressured to accept coaching or other co-curricular responsibilities. The organizational hierarchy of schools dictates that those with the least experience receive the most difficult schedule, the most poorly behaved students, and the worst space. This predictable pattern of Darwinian behavior on the part of senior teachers is problematic for the profession and damaging to students, yet I recognize that working conditions are difficult and professional survival is not a given. Years of working in compromised systems with few resources and demoralizing labor processes do drive some teachers to self-protection and isolation. Many researchers believe that unsupported induction and rigorous conditions through the first months and years are largely responsible for causing half of new teachers to leave within five years.

The literature is replete with studies that investigate teacher "attrition," blaming inadequate preparation, lack of authority, and less than ideal working conditions.[16] The few beginning teachers who start their careers in suburban schools with adequate space and textbooks, a desk for every student, an experienced staff, and grassy fields are not always successful in the transition to full-time teaching either. Teaching is not for the fainthearted and demands a focused, unswerving belief that almost all children can learn and that conventional schooling can support that learning. Teaching means providing an adequate education for the students without adequate resources. Teaching other people's children in a society that denigrates schooling, the poor, and teachers is not only powerful leadership, it is a form of activism.

Inhabiting the Role of Teacher

Into this challenging work culture steps each new class of reform-minded teachers, some of them young adults and others mid-career changers, all of them determined to make a difference. One of my colleagues describes why she chose a challenging school for her first job: "An equitable teacher is one who finds what each student needs and provides it for them, so each has an opportunity for success. A one-size-fits-all prescription is not the answer. My experience student teaching left me wanting to work in a place where student needs were least met, a place where assumptions and stereotypes held students from opportunities of success."

The majority of educators who become teachers and subsequently positional leaders were themselves successful in school. Many of those individuals may or may not have examined conflicting beliefs about the purposes of schooling in North America, particularly its role in the assimilation of foreigners. Few educators are students of Marx or study the history of formal education in this country. First-year teachers "re-enter" the school as emerging professionals, coming into a very familiar setting but sitting on the opposite side of the desk. Once they have reentered this familiar yet somewhat cloistered workplace, there is little time or incentive to fully interrogate the historical patterns that led to school as it is now construed. Ironically, teachers do stand on the front lines of the "war on poverty," as it was known in earlier times, and most believe formal education is the best medicine for the ills of societal inequality. Even as teachers are expected to solve the problems of an inherently inequitable society, however, they become handmaidens in an oppressive system that often reproduces inequity.

There are commonly held stereotypes about the worldliness of teachers compared to other professions, and they follow a continuum from socially committed individuals who wish to help others to the more derisive status of, "those who can't do, teach." Many who become schoolteachers, however intellectually competent, do represent a lower- and middle-economic class of individuals. "Schoolteaching," like ministry, social work, and nursing, has historically been one of the few professions open to working-class individuals, women, and first-generation Americans who may not speak English from birth. Unlike students pursuing higher-status professions of medicine and law, those who attended less prestigious public schools or now attend state colleges earn a teaching credential. There is a smaller percentage of teachers who come from middle-class backgrounds, and some report choosing teaching in spite of pressures from family and friends to choose a more lucrative line of work.

Choosing to Stay in Teaching

While I acknowledge the statistics about teacher attrition within the first five years of beginning the job, I question the use of the term *attrition* and the interpretation of that data. Many of these studies are based on sociological theories that treat teaching as a job like any other. The primary reasons teachers cite for "leaving" teaching are lack of professional support and poor working conditions. Most new teachers start in the least desirable work settings, meaning schools that serve low-income communities and are underresourced. Even with professional induction support programs and reasonable work settings, however, many teachers don't stay in the classroom. Within the four walls of a classroom, teachers are charged to mitigate the worst inequities of society, to disrupt historic discriminatory practices, and to create powerful learning environments based on their own vision of what schooling *could* be. Given the complexity of the work of teaching, it may take a few years for young teachers or mid-career changers to recognize the dilemmas created by great expectations and little autonomy and authority. Even with basic skills and growing competence, teaching is psychically and physically challenging. This work is not for everyone. Those who can will stay in teaching. Those who are not suited to the task move into other educational settings or different careers. The primary definition of *attrition* is a reduction or decrease in numbers, size, or strength. This connotation may be applicable here, but consider the second definition: a wearing down or weakening of resistance, especially as a result of continuous pressure or harassment. The pressures are relentless and demand integrity and leadership from those who stay.

Professional Identity Development

Fully inhabiting the role of teacher is a professional and personal odyssey requiring emotional and professional development that may be invisible to the teacher herself. These early years constitute a professional "identity-development" period, when young adults and some mid-career changers try out this complex and difficult role. Teachers come to the work from different standpoints. Some start out with a very clear idea of what the work is and who they are in the work, while others grow into the role and take longer to fully embrace the work. Some find the work overwhelming and unsatisfying, whatever they imagined the work of teaching to be. Members of this latter group should be supported in their decision to teach and lead in other settings or focus their interests in another direction. While all comers are challenged, only half prevail. I contend that surviving induction and finding success as a teacher is in itself a powerful act of leadership.

Educational leadership begins early in life and becomes more visible with the decision to enter the profession. The roots of teaching as a vocation are planted in childhood and adolescence, as teachers carry with them their own experiences as students. Teachers also report work experiences including coaching, tutoring, or just sharing one's interests and skills with others. Leadership activities continue throughout one's years in education, whatever the title, wherever the site, however the external world names and frames the work teachers do.

Teachers are sometimes assumed to have the same characteristics as their students. Those who teach the youngest children must therefore be the least worldly and sophisticated, as, for example, some observers see preschool teachers. Conversely, those who teach AP physics must be the smartest because they teach a "hard" subject. This characterization may seem beside the point, but consider how we judge leaders' competency. Is a person who works with five-year-olds a leader? While most teachers spend their days with human beings younger than themselves, their personalities cover the same breadth of brilliance and intellectual challenge as any other profession. Some music teachers are indeed temperamental artists, while others are quite concrete and stalwart. Some math teachers are very skilled at doing math, but not so skilled at making sure most of the kids learn it. Some high school teachers are very capable at instilling a love of literature in their students, yet find the role of department chair beyond their capacity. Grossman and Stodolsky[17] looked at secondary teachers' identities in relation to their subject areas and identified organizational differences within departments and status differences between departments. Disciplines do have status, and we judge others as representatives of their disciplines.

Images of Leading in Schools

Teachers also have identities in relation to their engagement with others in the workplace. Some are viewed, and view others, as team players who work effectively with positional leaders, while others avoid affiliation with administration.[18] I recall a conversation with another teacher during my first few years of teaching. This teacher had taught fine arts in junior high school for a very long time and laughed derisively when I told her I had been "elected" to the School Site Council. "Only a young, overly idealistic teacher would agree to such a request," said she. In her world, formal leadership and school governance were window dressing. "It doesn't matter who's up front," she said, impugning our current principal and the whole tribe of positional leaders. As that "overly idealistic" teacher, I was left wondering what school leadership was. I learned over time that leadership took many forms. Some teachers offered their leadership by serving students effectively, while others were more visible in governance and decision making. Some teachers shared their craft freely, bringing new colleagues into the guild much as craftsmen from the trades do. Others were brilliant thinkers and doers for a few years, then moved into other settings or roles. I learned that much of school leadership was provided by teachers. And I learned that taking leadership actions within the classroom was a requirement of the job.

Over the last thirty years, educational leaders have rediscovered collective, shared, distributed, or collaborative models of leading. Key influences on educational leadership reform include pressures on positional leaders to be instructional leaders, not just managers; pressures from teachers to retain or garner some measure of professional autonomy; and greater recognition that the quality of classroom instruction is central to improving student achievement. Approaching leadership by identifying what effective leaders actually do is also enlightening and offers potential for rethinking school leadership. For instance, "transformational leadership" represents movement from "transactional leadership."[19] Transactional leaders adapt to the culture of the organization, whereas transformational leaders strive to change the culture by engaging members in vision development. Leaders' values and the actions that portray those values are what matter most. If instructional expertise and cultural competence, or the ability to teach across difference, are essential to improving student achievement, then teachers are educational leaders with the greatest scope of influence. Educators who base practice on deep moral purpose are engaging in leadership, whatever the context.

Perceptions of the characteristics that make a leader are widely studied. One of my mentors, Linda Lambert, articulates the convergence between individual development, learning, and collaboration. Teachers lead in relationship with others, not as lone rangers. In this excerpt, she portrays leadership as learning well with others:

> When leadership means a person in a specific role enveloped in formal authority, teachers do not see themselves reflected in that image. When leadership becomes a broadly inclusive culture concept, it provokes a different response: I can see myself as participating in this learning work with my colleagues. Leadership realizes purpose, the sense of purpose that teachers brought with them into this profession.[20]

Lambert has studied adult learning for decades and believes that "leadership defined as a form of learning situates that work within the context of teaching and learning. So defined, it forms a sacred alliance among teaching, learning, and leading." She also addresses role and organizational context by adding, "The new language of leadership, accompanied by assumptions about who can learn and who can lead, frame the foundation for an evocative context for teacher leadership. The most vital aspect of this new definition lies in its relationship to learning."[21] Lambert connects leadership to organizational change, transformation of followers, and a community of leaders. She states the following:

These movements have paved the way for some evocative assumptions about leadership. It is suggested that those assumptions could be summarized as:

1. Leadership may be understood as reciprocal, purposeful learning in community.

2. Everyone has the right, responsibility and capability to be a leader.

3. The adult learning environment in the school and district is the most critical factor in evoking leadership identities and actions.

4. Within that environment, opportunities for skillful participation top the list of priorities.

5. How we define leadership frames how people will participate.

6. Educators are purposeful—leading realizes purpose.[22]

Lambert's integration of constructivist learning and leading, attention to collegial interactions, and attention to organizational culture offer a framework to understand the complex interactions among these dimensions. Leadership is "situated" rather than inherent. Taking action from a foundation of moral purpose is reflected in her depiction and the following work as well.

Mendez-Morse's review of leadership literature identifies the following six characteristics of leaders of educational change:

- Having vision
- Believing that the schools are for learning
- Valuing human resources
- Being a skilled communicator and listener
- Acting proactively
- Taking risks[23]

Any individual, whether principal, teacher, or parent leader, can reflect such characteristics. Notions of who can be a leader, therefore, must continually be revisited with careful attention to characteristics of leading, rather than personality traits. Educational leadership happens at all levels, in every dimension of the teaching and learning enterprise, every day. Embracing teaching as leadership allows us to rethink schooling, leadership, and school reform.

Leadership Roles in and Beyond the Classroom

Educational leadership begins in the classroom and moves outward. In subsequent chapters, I describe school leadership from the teacher's perspective. Teachers learn about leadership throughout life and from many sources—but begin careers as school leaders in the classroom. Starting with the values and purposes teachers bring into the profession, I consider the ways teachers lead and the evolution of leadership development from the classroom outward. Placing instructional leadership at the center of school leadership, I follow my colleagues through their journeys as teachers leading. Descriptions of why they chose the work of teaching are followed by examples of classroom-based instruction as leadership. Teachers describe their relationship to others and how to work effectively with role-alike and task-alike groups of colleagues. They describe the challenges and benefits of working across difference to build relationships, gain trust, and effect change in their classrooms, schools, and beyond.

Advocacy for students and improved instruction leads predictably to schoolwide leadership. At the school level, individual teachers share expertise and seek professional support from others. Specialized knowledge is strengthened by affiliation with professional groups and advanced training, deepening knowledge about particular content, pedagogy, and practices. Teachers carry hard-won expertise back to professional organizations, bartering trade secrets and improving practice. Teachers lead by reaching out to the communities they serve, whether friends and neighbors who support schooling, parents of their students, or professionals from other work settings who can support them in the quest to bring learning to students.

The historic and cultural roots of school leadership are deep. Examine through new eyes the places and spaces where you lead and your students learn, within and beyond the school. Consider leadership *actions*, rather than title or role. Think about the work of teaching in all its dimensions, and about what kinds of leadership actions are embedded in that work. Understand clearly what and who we are as a profession and how we came to be this way. Education is ever-changing, even though some of our practices aren't evolving as quickly as our students are. Teachers are building the future of education by bringing the wisdom of practice to educational leadership.

Historical and Cultural Influences on Leadership

Precedent for School Leadership Form and Function

- Remember site leaders are required to manage, and most instructional leadership takes place in classrooms.
- Recognize where and how site leaders influence and support adult and student learning, and build on that influence and support.

- Appreciate the power of instructional leadership in the classroom, at the grade level and department, and beyond. Strengthen connections between people and across roles.

Places and Spaces Where Teachers Lead

- Be conscious of where your ideas of formal leadership come from.
- Listen to your descriptions of what "leaders" do and what you do. Use purposeful language to characterize who and what you are as a leader.
- Take a good look at your facility and the ways in which the spaces shape practice.
- Recognize the power of your experience and bring what you know into the mainstream of the reform conversation.

✑ INQUIRY ONE ✑
Leadership Activities

A Week (or a Month) in the Life of a Teacher

Purpose: To capture data that shows you when, where, and how you lead.

Recasting the work of teaching as leading requires a systematic description of the work of teaching in all its forms. The physical structure of the "egg carton" school, where teachers go into the classroom with the students in the morning and come out of that same space for periodic breaks and at the end of the day is a powerful organizing feature of the work. Even though teachers devote a certain amount of time to adult interactions, the primary image of teaching is standing in front of students. To help you flesh out this image with the many forms of leadership you engage in every day, take some data about how, when, and with whom you interact on a daily, weekly, and monthly basis.

Keep a log of activities for one week or one month (see the sample logs in Exhibits 1.1 and 1.2). Start on Sunday and

Exhibit 1.1. Weekly Log

	Sun	Mon	Tues	Wed	Thurs	Fri	Sat
Before school							
8:00							
9:00							
10:00							
11:00							
12:00							
1:00							
2:00							
3:00							
After school							
Evening							

Exhibit 1.2. Monthly Log of Meetings, Contacts, and Other Outreach or Professional Activity

	Week 1	Week 2	Week 3	Week 4
Before school				
Mornings				
Noon or midday				
After school				
Evenings				

include any planning, grading, or other prep activity. For each hour, activity, or period, note the activity, educational purpose, and any individuals with whom you interact.

Analysis of a Week or a Month in the Life of a Teacher

When do you interact with colleagues?

What is the purpose of those interactions? Are they planned, formal, or informal?

Do you come early each day to prepare, or do you do more preparation during breaks or after school?

How many of your interactions involve staff, teachers, specialists, parents, or others?

Are there patterns to your week or month that can be strengthened or changed to support your work?

Where do leadership actions appear within those events, exchanges, and conversations?

The Physical Characteristics of Schools Shape Teaching, Learning, and Leadership

Put on your anthropologist hat and look at your school as if for the first time. Imagine you are coming onto the grounds as a traveler from another country.

Describe the Building and Its Occupants

Draw a schematic of the school, including all classroom wings, offices, the gym, cafeteria, and portables. For multiple stories, show each level.

Label by grade, department, or function.

With a partner from a different site, discuss the implications of the layout.

How does the facility support or inhibit physical interactions between adults? For example, a large school with multiple wings might cluster by grade level or department or might mix the grade levels (with all bilingual or "gifted" classes in one wing, K–5).

Critical Reflection Questions

Where are the different classes and functions in relation to the office? For instance, the office might be at one end of the grounds on one side of the parking lot, while the classroom wings are on the other side of the parking lot.

What is the quality of classroom space for different groups? For instance, the special education students are in a deteriorating portable in the parking lot, while other students are near the office.

What messages does the organization of the facility send to students, staff, families, and visitors?

Is the facility equitably shared by all members of the community? Which groups have the most desirable space?

What is the history of this particular organizational scheme? Is it still relevant? Can or should it be changed?

The School in the Community

Is this school a community center?

Who uses it, and when, and how?

What policies are in place to create a welcoming atmosphere to "regular" occupants and visitors, affiliated groups, and other groups?

What is the enrollment policy (neighborhood, open enrollment, magnet, or selective admissions)?

Resources

Frost, D., Durrant, J., Head, M., and Holden, G., *Teacher-Led School Improvement* (New York: RoutledgeFalmer, 2000).

Frost and his coauthors describe the ways teachers in Great Britain needed to "rebuild teacher professionalism" in the face of nationalizing the curriculum. The authors and participants recognize the many roles of leadership teachers play and the importance of teacher expertise in the midst of reform. The section on teacher-led inquiry is especially useful.

Hall, P., and Simeral, A., *Building Teachers' Capacity for Success* (Alexandria, Va.: ASCD, 2008).

This book was coauthored by a school principal and a literacy coach and focuses on the stages of developing collaboration. The stage development approach offers some useful ideas to readers, particularly those new to facilitation of professional development. There are links to downloadable forms.

Institute for Educational Leadership, *Leadership for Student Learning: Redefining Teacher Leadership—a Report on the Task Force of Teacher Leadership* (Washington, D.C.: Institute for Educational Leadership, 2001).

This report makes a case for teacher leadership, examining the difficulties teachers face as leaders in schools. Drawing from school change and school leadership literature, the report makes recommendations about what needs to change in schools as organizations for teachers to function as professionals and lead needed change. It's not a how-to text by any means, but it is a well-crafted over-view of schooling practices that continue to hamper student success.

Katzenmeyer, M., and Moller, G., *Awakening the Sleeping Giant: Helping Teachers Develop as Leaders*, 3rd ed. (Thousand Oaks, Calif.: Corwin Press, 2009).

> Now in its third edition, this text continues to serve a broad range of teacher leadership audiences. The authors give well-researched definitions of teacher leadership, offer a range of self-study and facilitator-friendly activities, and stay grounded in the real world of school reform. As one reviewer noted, the authors have stayed abreast of the evolving world of teacher leadership.

Lambert, L., *Leadership Capacity for Lasting School Improvement* (Alexandria, Va.: ASCD, 2003).

> Lambert's text is a wonderful synthesis of her career-long interest in school leadership. She focuses on skillful leadership by all members of the school community, rather than focusing on what one skillful leader does. The tools and surveys for analysis are useful as conversation starters, data collectors, and program evaluation frameworks.

McGhan, B., "A Fundamental Education Reform: Teacher-Led Schools," *Phi Delta Kappan* 83(7) (2002): 538–540.

> There are few accessible articles about teacher-led schools, and this is one. The author outlines key conflicts in school leadership roles, for instance, revisiting the challenge for principals to be true instructional leaders when what's actually needed is principals who are good managers. He describes wholesale change efforts versus incremental change and points out that teacher leadership is the key factor in either case.

Murphy, J., *Connecting School Leadership and School Improvement* (Thousand Oaks, Calif.: Corwin Press, 2005).

> This text gathers, synthesizes, and describes research on teacher leadership. It's not an easy read or a how-to,

but it is a good reference and provides detailed context for readers who want to delve into theories of leadership, teacher leadership, and school improvement.

The Project on the Next Generation of Teachers, Harvard Graduate School of Education.
www.gse.harvard.edu/~ngt/papers.htm

Susan Moore Johnson and her team address "critical questions about the future of the nation's teaching force" through a series of studies about the teaching profession. Their research on "second-stage teachers" is especially instructive in understanding teacher professionalism and teacher leadership.

York-Barr, J., and Duke, K., "What Do We Know About Teacher Leadership? Findings from Two Decades of Scholarship," *Review of Educational Research* 74(3) (2004): 255–316.

This is a review of the literature about teacher leadership research over two decades. The researchers describe the kinds of studies and various findings about what teacher leadership is, the forms it takes, conditions that influence it, and characteristics of teacher leaders. The researchers acknowledge that "the construct of teacher leadership is not well defined." This would be useful for those in professional development and teachers conducting self-study of the work of teaching.

Notes

The epigraph to this chapter is drawn from R. P. Warren, *The Legacy of the Civil War: Meditations on the Centennial* (Cambridge, Mass.: Harvard University Press, 1983; originally published 1961).

1. E. Condliffe Lagemann, "The Plural Worlds of Educational Research," *History of Education Quarterly* Summer (1989).

2. L. Beck and J. Murphy, *Understanding the Principalship: Metaphorical Themes, 1920s–1990s* (New York: Teachers College Press, 1993).

3. National Center for Education Statistics, *The Condition of Education: Contexts of Elementary and Secondary Education* (Washington, D.C.: National Center for Education Statistics, 2009).

4. W. N. Grubb and J. Flessa, "'A Job Too Big for One': Multiple Principals and Other Nontraditional Approaches to School Leadership," *Educational Administration Quarterly* 42 (2006): 518–550.

5. A. Etzioni, *The Semi-Professions and Their Organization: Teachers, Nurses, Social Workers*, ed. A. Etzioni (New York: Free Press, 1969); I. F. Goodson and A. Hargreaves, *Teachers' Professional Lives* (London: Falmer Press, 1996); D. Lortie, *Schoolteacher* (Chicago: University of Chicago Press, 1975).

6. L. Cherubini, "A Grounded Theory Analysis of Beginning Teachers' Experiences: Illuminating Leadership Capacities," *International Journal of Teacher Leadership* 1(1) (2008); M. Collay, "Discerning Professional Identity and Becoming Bold, Socially Responsible Teacher Leaders," *Educational Leadership and Administration: Teaching and Program Development* 18 (2006): 131–146.

7. J. W. Little, "The Persistence of Privacy: Autonomy and Initiative in Teachers' Professional Relations," *Teachers College Record* 91(4) (1990): 509–536.

8. D. Shantz and P. Prieur, "Teacher Professionalism and School Leadership: An Antithesis?" *Education* 116 (1996): 393–396.

9. T. Hallett, "The Leadership Struggle: The Case of Costen Elementary School," in *Distributed Leadership in Practice*, eds. J. Spillane and J. Diamond (New York: Teachers College Press, 2007).

10. A. Hargreaves, "Contrived Collegiality: The Micropolitics of Teacher Collaboration," in *The Politics of Life in Schools: Power, Conflict and Cooperation*, ed. J. Blasé (London: Sage, 1991).

11. J. Flessa, "Education Micropolitics and Distributed Leadership," *Peabody Journal of Education* 84 (2009): 331–349.

12. M. H. Metz, "How Social Class Differences Shape Teachers' Work," in *The Contexts of Teaching in Secondary Schools: Teachers' Realities*, eds. M. W. McLaughlin, J. E. Talbert, and N. Bascia (New York: Teachers College Press, 1994).

13. J. Kafka, "The Principalship in Historical Perspective," *Peabody Journal of Education* 84 (2009).

14. D. Ravitch, *The Death and Life of the Great American School System: How Testing and Choice Are Undermining Education* (New York: Basic Books, 2010).

15. National Commission on Excellence in Education, "A Nation at Risk: The Imperative for Educational Reform" (Washington, D.C.: National Commission on Excellence in Education, 1983).

16. "Teacher Attrition: A Costly Loss to the Nation and to the States." *Alliance for Excellence in Education* August (2005).

17. P. Grossman and S. Stokolsky, "Content as Context: The Role of School Subjects in Secondary School Teaching," *Educational Researcher* 24(8) (1995): 5–23.

18. S. M. Johnson and M. L. Donaldson, "Overcoming the Obstacles to Leadership," *Educational Leadership* 64(1) (2007): 8–13.

19. J. Stewart, "Transformational Leadership: An Evolving Concept Examined Through the Works of Burns, Bass, Avolio, and Leithwood," *Canadian Journal of Educational Administration and Policy* 54 (2006).

20. L. Lambert, "Leadership Redefined: An Evocative Context for Teacher Leadership," *School Leadership and Management* 23(4) (2003): 421–430.

21. Lambert, "Leadership Redefined," 425.

22. Lambert, "Leadership Redefined," 425.

23. S. Mendez-Morse, *Leadership Characteristics That Facilitate School Change* (Austin, Tex.: SEDL, 1992). www.sedl.org/change/leadership.

2

THE PERSONAL DIMENSIONS
OF LEADERSHIP

I pray for all of us the strength to teach our children
what they must learn, and the humility and wisdom
to learn from them so that we might teach better.

—*Lisa Delpit*

To fully understand teaching as leading, it is essential to embrace the personal dimensions of school leadership. The values we bring into the classroom reflect our beliefs about who we are and what it means to teach. When school leadership is cast as management, school leaders' primary roles are managing staff, facilities, and materials. Teachers teach, principals manage. The relentless demands of twenty-first-century schooling require educators to provide extensive social and academic support, affecting both instructional and management responsibilities in schools. Teaching and managing require leadership. Teachers are not line workers reporting to a supervisor and punching the clock at the end of the shift. For schools to be places where learning takes place, the work of teaching and learning with students, families, and colleagues must be recognized as leadership. Teaching with integrity grows out of a lifetime of experience as a learner and leader. This chapter explores the life experiences of teachers that influenced their decisions to become teachers, the personal dimensions of teaching, and the ways teachers inhabit their roles after they enter the classroom.

Positional leaders—whether principals, teacher leaders, instructional coaches, or anyone identified as a teacher with a specialty—are most often charged to guide instructional leadership and implement complex school reform efforts. That professional work, however, is done by teachers, whether within classrooms, grade-level teams, departments, or at the district level and beyond. Artifacts of the factory model of schooling, where the principal distributed students and materials to multiple classrooms, may linger. Expanding the principal's role to include "instructional leader" is well intended, but even a great teacher turned principal cannot "lead instruction" in every classroom. Real learning happens because of what teachers and students create together in the classroom. Curriculum is not just the content found between two covers of a book. Rather, teachers and students—in accord with other adults at school, parents, and community—run the course together. Teacher beliefs about the purposes of schooling influence practice within the classroom, throughout the school, and beyond the school to the larger community. This path to creating conditions for student learning leads individuals to take leadership actions at all levels.

The National Commission on Teaching and America's Future[1] (NCTAF) focuses on standards-based teacher preparation and professional development. It cites three premises, the first of which is: "What teachers know and can do is the most important influence on what students learn." We know that few schools or school systems are structured to support this substantial acknowledgement, functioning for the most part as they have for one hundred years. In spite of organizational and professional hindrances, however, competent teachers strive to create productive classroom-based learning for students. Committed teachers working on behalf of student learning bring all aspects of life experience and professional knowledge into the classroom and the school. NCTAF's second premise affirms that "recruiting, preparing, and retaining good teachers is the central strategy for improving our schools." This text may illuminate one of the reasons why teachers choose or are chosen to teach. NCTAF's final premise is frequently overlooked and undervalued: "school reform cannot succeed unless it focuses on creating the conditions in which teachers can teach, and teach well." Schools are not easy places to work. Teaching well, whatever the conditions, is a powerful form of leadership. When the many facets of teaching are acknowledged, leadership is evident throughout every dimension of practice. In this chapter, I consider the personal dimensions of school leadership, where teaching and learning are at the core of the enterprise.

What teachers know begins with our own experiences in school and the larger society. While renewed recognition of the importance of teacher quality is encouraging, philosophers have debated the meaning of the verb *to know* for millennia. As teachers, we need to know content, how to teach it, and how to fully engage twenty to forty individual learners. That knowledge is not offered in textbooks or a course on classroom management. Pedagogical competence is not separate from our beliefs and values. Where do our beliefs about teaching, learning, and leading come from?

Teaching as a Vocation

Whether individuals identify teaching as a calling before they change sides of the desk, most who stay in teaching will in some fashion characterize their work as a "vocation," similar to ministry. *Vocation* derives from the Latin root *vocare*, to call or to be called. New teachers don't arrive at their first assignment prepared only with a formal education. Intertwined throughout our own schooling histories is a profusion of learning and leading experiences that inform how we think of the role of teacher. Each of us carries vivid images of what teachers do. Beliefs about teachers and teaching come from our own schooling experiences, media, family lore, and other community and work histories.[2] At various points throughout childhood or young adulthood, many of us were mentored or coached by adults who themselves had made a commitment to providing leadership for young people. Inchoate notions of what it means to be a teacher are influenced by these early experiences, and they powerfully shape our "teacher selves."

Teaching is not just another job. Choosing to work with children and youth on a daily basis is sometimes elevated to superhuman status. As a neighbor of mine states, "I could never do what you do." Simultaneously, teaching has been delegated to the working class and to women who were previously unable to attain work in higher-status professions. Teaching has been portrayed as a job for individuals who want to keep the same hours as their children or a temporary stopgap job to build a résumé or until something better comes along. I find this characterization unfortunate and hardly representative of the majority of the profession. One need only teach side by side with someone who is not fully engaged in this calling to understand the difficulty they create for themselves and their students. While some veteran teachers become disillusioned and burned out, it is unfair to assume this group dominates the profession.

Teachers often start in other professions and then choose the classroom as a better environment for their gifts. Study in other social sciences, for example, provides a strong foundation for teaching. Annamarie, a third-grade teacher, came into the profession in her midthirties after other work experience and undertaking graduate study in a related field:

> While working on my masters in psychology, I decided that I preferred to pursue a teaching job to inspire and connect with kids in a school setting. I continue to have a great interest in philosophy and social justice issues. I believe that psychology and philosophy are at the core of teaching. I am grateful I have followed this path. I feel blessed every day I go to work, because I have so much fun teaching. I get so much joy doing it, it is not work, it is a passion!

Whether any of us teach children or adults for a few months or a lifetime, the work of teaching is a deeply human endeavor.

Whether we believe our primary function is to build relationships with kindergarten children or to ensure that high school students learn about great novelists, teaching isn't telling. The craft of teaching is developed over a lifetime, requiring practitioners to draw upon life experiences, pedagogical knowledge, and a desire to ensure that students leave our classrooms with something of value.

Once embedded in the bureaucracy, teachers may struggle to recall the vocation they imagined in their youth or while toiling in another profession wishing for work that was more fulfilling. Once we fully understand the requirements and the psychic cost, however, most who don't feel the call will move on to different work. Those with the courage to stay, however, may reconcile the challenges of accepting the call to teach. We are encouraged and appreciated by students and families, colleagues who share our values, and our own family members. Teachers who continue to find fulfillment and remain in the classroom have a strong constitution and a great capacity to maintain integrity. We often have family members who are themselves teachers or who at least commit to supporting us. For many, teaching is a family enterprise where conversations at home include discussing challenges and successes, sharing professional lore, and networking.

Instilling Values While Remaining Neutral

From colonial times through the 1960s, teachers were by law expected to parent students to some degree, standing "in loco parentis" (in the place of parents) as part of their role. Under this principle that dates back to English common law, teachers were expected not only to teach content, but to discipline students and imbue appropriate moral standards. Public schools became more secular over the twentieth century, however, putting greater emphasis on teacher as instructor and less emphasis on teacher as moral guide. Expectations of contemporary teachers remain conflicted. Teachers can't spend thirty-five to fifty hours a week with children and young people and not accept some responsibility for moral, civic, and community education. Public school teachers are not allowed by professional standards and common practice to proselytize, invite, or encourage students to embrace specific religious beliefs or political stances. Teachers are, however, expected to model civic responsibility, good social conduct, and collegiality. Teachers are expected to be "good role models." At the same time, teachers are not allowed to openly discuss where those values come from, whether political, religious, or secular. This modern role confusion is not always recognized as a values conflict, although cultural differences between teachers and the communities where they teach are legend. Attempts to standardize behavioral expectations of students are codified to some degree by programs like Second Step and Caring School Community that formalize the role of schooling in general and teachers in particular for shaping the behavior of students. Current attention to bullying in schools, for example, reflects the greater societal belief that school staffs *should* "parent" students, and teachers are in fact expected to monitor student behavior.

Teaching is one of the "helping" professions. Those who enter the profession because they are excited about a field of study and seek to instill young people with the same excitement soon learn that just presenting material about that topic is not sufficient or even passable teaching. Children and young people are relational beings, and they seek connection to a caring adult who at least sees and hears them. Creating an environment where students can learn is custodial, parental, and social. Without some care for the other, teaching and learning is limited at best and damaging at worst. Humane teaching is characterized as an "ethic of care" by feminist philosophers who believe that caring for the other is requisite to teaching.[3] Noguera considers the role of "teacher care" in his examination of school violence.[4] Many teachers invest heavily in building relationships with students to strengthen the teaching and learning environment. There is a healthy debate about this stance, of course, within and beyond school settings. While a few teachers believe the job description doesn't include emotional nurturance, most of us understand that part of the work of teaching is to provide a caring, supportive learning environment for the child, youth, or adult learner. On a more practical plane, teaching requires mediating educational access for the next generation of humans, and acquiring new learning requires emotional and intellectual sustenance. Following is an example of the breadth of roles one teacher brings to her students.

> Mona is a special education teacher at a middle school. Through a "focus student" inquiry (a case study), she reported on one of her students and the effects of her awareness of the student's home life on her assessment and recommendations. Her expertise reflects attention to the student's family background, academic history, and current needs. In her analysis, Mona describes Leah, a twelve-year-old sixth-grade student who "lives with her parents, a twin brother, and an older brother." This student "has attended school in this district since kindergarten," indicating she is familiar with the student's records and academic history. Leah's "primary language is Spanish, and it is spoken in the home."
>
> Mona outlines the student's learning disabilities, including "weaknesses in auditory memory, auditory processing, and visual processing skills." She outlines specific services she and others have provided the student and gives examples of her current performance, such as "she is able to write a complete sentence with adequate punctuation. . . . Has extreme difficulty spelling and poor penmanship." Finally, Mona offers a glimpse into Leah's social-emotional status, indicating that Leah "is a determined student and always gives her best effort." Mona describes Leah's behavior in small groups, larger classes, with peers, and with adults.

Mona not only uses technical and developmentally sound expertise, she also demonstrates care for the child and her life circumstances. While teachers can't write a detailed case history on every student, most teachers inform their teaching practices with knowledge of individual student circumstances.

The Cultural Roots of Our Practice

"What teachers know" about schooling is drawn from life experiences as students and members of communities. Our own memories of school are composed of successes, challenges, and conflicts that inspire us to take actions on behalf of students and families. Students experience schooling as a cross-cultural process, even if they represent a racial majority in their school. In this example from a university course, Leticia relates: "I say this from experience. I had some professors who told me that I should not be in school, that I was not going to learn anything, and that I was not doing well in school because I was 'Mexican,' and Mexican students are not as smart as Asian students."

A mid-career mother of adult children and bilingual teacher, Leticia recalled painful memories of exclusion from the U.S. higher education system. Many teachers of color tell a similar story, especially if they are the first in their family to go to college. "Fortunately for me, I had the trust, guidance, and support from teachers and mentors who challenged the system and helped me go through college. Hopefully, I can make a difference for my students." Leticia and her colleagues established a parent education center at their school and created a series of parent education events to build stronger relationships between school and home.

Very few of us who survive the educational system, whether pre-K–12 or higher education, recall complete acceptance. Teachers who come from immigrant families, speak English as a second language, or are socially marginalized in other ways bring specialized knowledge about how unwelcoming school can be for children from backgrounds like theirs. Leticia has integrated those life experiences into a powerful form of advocacy leadership at her school. Her white colleague and parent education partner said this to her: "You are a true leader. You show respect to all, but you have your eye on the needs of our students. You move others towards action through your example. You help me see the world through a lens not available before. And you lead in a caring, focused way."

Teachers who were successful without much mentoring may recall a dearth of personal support and choose a different path when they are in the position to do so. A teacher who was a very successful high school student had her choices limited by school-based adults as she sought access to higher education. Estelle recalls "knowing there were counselors at our school— they had a designated wing. Not once did I meet with them or did they tell me the options or requirements for college." She noted other "gatekeepers" along the way, whose presence she attributed to her race: "Being a minority and having been raised first-generation Mexican American, no one in my family had ever been to college. The most education anyone in my family had was junior high, maybe some high school. So this concept of higher education was foreign and confusing." Estelle's story is common among people who are the first in their families to go to college, and many teachers are the first generation in their family to attend college. They bring a degree of cross-cultural competence that informs their teaching and schoolwide leadership. Estelle continues making connections to her own experience:

> I always knew I was a smart student. I was always on honor roll and received many awards. But that's just because I was raised to respect teachers and to always follow their rules, complete my homework, respect others. I always followed strictly by the book,

because that's how I was taught at home. In retrospect, I consider myself very fortunate to have been raised the way I was, because otherwise I am not sure that I would have gotten into a four-year university right out of high school.

Estelle makes the connection between her own experience, when she lacked information on prerequisites for college, and what the school should do for students:

There could be a variety of factors that may contribute to gate-keeping. However, it is the school's responsibility to equally inform or to even inform at all the parents and students of the community they serve about college requirements. It is then up to each family to make their own educated choices about the courses their student can enroll in.

Estelle's choice of words is instructive, as she outlines her thinking that "it is up to each family to make their own edu-cated choices." Education is "knowing what your options are or knowing what your children's options are." Some families bring their children to school with little or no formal second-ary or higher education, and it is the school's job to tell them about the options. Estelle knows that without accurate and timely information about how students gain access to the educa-tional process, families cannot advocate for their children's best interests. As a teacher, she leads by recognizing the inequity of the system, and she is committed to opening gates and creating access for others in her community:

It is too late for me to roll back the hands of time, but as I con-tinue to climb that ladder of higher education, I take on the responsibility to inform others within my family and community about how gatekeeping works and warn them about the actions they may take. I can only wonder what college courses I could have taken if I had participated in some AP courses when I was in high school.

These teachers reveal how their own life influences their practice as educational leaders and shapes their understanding of the role of the teacher and the school. They articulate an advocacy stance that informs how they work within the school for the community. Their "calling" is to serve as advocates for the newest entrants to the educational system.

Teaching "in Loco Parentis" (in Place of Parents)

Debates about the purpose of schooling in modern times emerge from very significant philosophical differences. When schooling moved out of homes and churches into multi-community and cross-cultural settings, dilemmas arose about what would be taught and who would do the teaching. If teaching and learning is indeed a moral and social enterprise, teachers will naturally imbue students with certain values. Every act of teaching is an expression of beliefs that guide our practice. Whether human beings are naturally good or naturally bad may not be articulated in such stark terms, but every decision teachers make is based on personal convictions about the human condition. Unexamined assumptions about the purpose of schooling often leave teachers in the position of mediating conflicting values between self and other, child and parent, or school and community. Even when these big ideas about the purpose of education aren't addressed directly, they influence our practice, and our actions reveal our philosophy. Making our values transparent and acting on them is risk-laden and an act of leadership. /

I believe we craft our practice along a continuum of beliefs about the purposes of formal education and make decisions that reflect our beliefs about the complex processes of teaching and learning. Our leadership is challenged in myriad ways while we run the course together, usually finding the journey a steeplechase rather than a sprint. Few of us fall at one end of the continuum or the other, but we strive each day to enact our values with integrity, if not always with elegance. Teachers who believe that one of the purposes of schooling is to develop democratic citizens will start the day with a class meeting and assign classroom chores, while teachers who believe content is king will focus more on dispensing information. Teachers who accept that some degree of co-parenting is part of teaching children will include formal instruction about manners, personal hygiene, and peer interactions. Others assert it is the parents' responsibility, not the teacher's, to raise the children and manage social skills and will act accordingly.

Conflicts Between Parent Values and Teacher Values

Children and young people need teachers and other adults to hold them accountable for their behavior, yet conflict arises when there is disagreement about the standard of behavior. Teacher and parent ultimately must partner for learning to occur, whether we are teaching values or the multiplication tables. Whatever the balance of task and individual development, the adult in charge has many roles to play, including leader, manager, instructor, disciplinarian, and cheerleader. The job that is also a calling requires disciplinary knowledge, child development expertise, and tactful interactions with children, families, and colleagues on a daily basis. Teachers plan instruction for a large group, but every child or young person comes with a different way of learning. When I talk with colleagues about how they balance the needs of individuals against the needs of the group, I learn again how challenging the work of reaching every child is. They describe drawing on knowledge about child development, using social or family-provided information, and their own observations of a child's social behavior to modify instruction. Here is the report of an experienced fourth-grade teacher, Lisbeth, who fully embraces the parenting part teaching:

> Sarah is a shy student overall, but volunteers to answer questions and read aloud in class. She made friends quickly this year and has told me she feels more accepted at this school than at

her previous school. Socially she fits in with all of her peers. She tried out for the basketball team this year, which really helped with her self-confidence. When she was younger, she had trouble separating herself from her mom at the beginning of the day and often cried and became extremely emotional. According to her mother, this behavior has decreased as she has matured, but she still wanted me to be aware that Sarah worries a lot about her family. She hasn't exhibited any of that behavior this year.

This level of detail may not be documented in most cases, but many teachers have this level of knowledge about their students. The report captures the essence of a teacher and parent collaborating on behalf of a child's success at school.

How Parenting Informs Teaching

What teachers know about child development comes from professional knowledge, disciplinary knowledge, and our own parenting practices. Many teachers report a maturing of practice after becoming parents, now having first-hand experience about raising children and sending them off to school. In the following excerpt, Tony describes his challenges balancing work and family, articulating in detail how the multiple roles inform each other:

When I think of my flurry of daily activity, foremost in my thoughts are my three school-aged children. Parenting, teaching, and leadership are tightly interwoven in my life. It is a constant juggling act in which each informs the other, and each strengthens the other. This is my challenge: to maintain the attitude that each of these facets complements the other.

Tony and I met many times in his classroom after school, where sometimes one or another of his children was doing homework while he graded papers and planned instruction for the next day. He spoke of the challenge of trying to do it all: "At home with my children I share about experiences in the classroom and in the university. In the classroom, I share about experiences with my children—often with a comical edge." In his development as a leader, Tony made the connections within the leadership program classes. "By the time I get to the university, I cannot help but share what is happening in my home life, school life, and how it all relates to leadership." He continued to make the connections about how one part of his life informs another, stating: "I have learned that my skills as a parent are often the selfsame skills used in the realms of teaching and leadership." This dinner-table vignette captures the intersection of teaching, leading, and parenting at Tony's house:

> Before we get on to "small talk," I discipline myself to ask specific questions about assignments due the next day and about long-term assignments. I typically say, "Johnny, estimate how much time it will take for you to finish your work due tomorrow. Which subjects do you still have to work on?" I go through the same list of questions with each child. If it looks like most of their work is done, I gauge their energy level and ask if they could spend fifteen or thirty minutes on long-term projects. We go over due dates and negotiate reasonable workloads.

I imagine Tony makes the same decisions for himself during the work day. He brings expertise about how schoolwork should go from his professional setting to his home. He has set priorities and a standard of academic excellence for his own children. Tony describes mixing and matching study breaks, use of electronic games, and not having cable television. "I am wearing my leadership hat when I employ skills like asking specific questions, time management, and negotiation. I take this way of approaching people and tasks into the classroom and beyond."

Educational leadership comes in many forms and, as Tony describes, in multiple settings. He thinks about it at home while parenting his own children, at school coaching students and colleagues, and at the university, where he has undertaken a graduate degree in educational leadership. His reflection captures the powerful influence of parenting on teaching.

Many of us are both parents and teachers. Those of us who work as urban educators may have conflicting feelings about our own children's education. We believe schools are the last best hope for creating a democracy, yet we may avoid the local schools because we feel compelled to find the "best" education for our own children. This tension sometimes places parents who are teachers in the uncomfortable position of not enrolling their own children in the district where they teach or live. We must continue to ask ourselves the question: Would I want my child to attend this school? That question leads us to set the highest standard for our practice as leaders. Carol reflects on her development as a leader and makes this connection between parenting and leadership:

> I hope I have become a better listener and more observant about how I am present to staff, parents and students. In my daily actions and words, I try to make our school the inclusive, inviting community I would want for my own children.

Our standards for what makes a good education come to some degree from parenting and striving to create communities for learners that could support our most important client. In this last example, Tom aligns his goals as an educator with his perspectives as a parent:

> I believe in public education that is inclusive of the community. I think that schools should include parents as much as possible and reflect positive community values. To me, this means respecting the home language and culture of the student. This includes respecting the civil rights of all students. I would want the school where I work to be a place where I would send my own children. It should be a safe place where learning is going on at all levels.

Teaching as a Profession

I believe that the tensions we feel about whether teaching is a true profession reside in the challenges to reconcile the moral dimensions of teaching with the intellectual and technical dimensions of teaching. Sociologists characterize teaching as a "semi-profession." They argue that a "true" profession is characterized by a body of knowledge, techniques, and specific training, a service orientation, and distinctive ethics that support self-regulation. Teaching as a fully recognized profession would have status similar to law and medicine.[5] Teachers do not yet set common professional standards and lack autonomy and authority to hire and fire. Teachers have more authority within the instructional role, even within the current culture of reform du jour. Fortunately, most of us think of ourselves as professionals and hold ourselves to a high standard. Almost all of us undertake a postbaccalaureate course of study and internship and continue to develop competency and skill over a lifetime. We are committed to ensuring our students learn, whether we have institutional support, resources, or recognition of the challenges we encounter. We conduct formal inquiry and applied research in the classroom and school to improve practice, and we collaborate with our colleagues to build the strength of the entire staff. As a mid-career teacher completing graduate work in educational leadership reflects,

> This inquiry has given me an acute awareness of how educational practices and policy affect a school community. I believe that finding solutions requires reaching out and creating dialogue with key stakeholders. Leaders must push beyond their comfort zones and seek, prod, ask, and answer questions about policies and practices in order to find solutions. It's only through dialogue that change can begin to occur.

Lisa, another mid-career teacher and a senior member of her staff, reflected on her graduate education, acknowledging actions taken and future plans. She addresses the centrality of relationships between members of the community in this way:

I need to continue to plant seeds of positive connections between parents, staff, and families and explore ways to include veteran teachers in a positive way. I want to learn ways to resolve conflicts that arise between different cultures. I feel especially challenged when conflicts arise between families of color and veteran teachers, or between conservative and progressive staff members.

Another teacher considering a role change to the vice principalship described her grade-level team leadership in curriculum reform. After leading her team through a multiple-year process of refining math and writing assessments, Terry relates:

Professional development is also important to ongoing growth and lifelong learning. I have been fortunate to have the opportunity to work with teachers through a mathematics adoption. As a trainer, I have worked with third- and fourth-grade teachers on how to best use the adopted materials to improve math achievement of all their students, especially their at-risk, underperforming students.

Each of these teachers articulates concepts of professionalism through commitment to students, their colleagues, and their pedagogy. Their values are clearly stated, and they offer many examples of how those values inform their leadership as teachers. In the next excerpt, a mid-career teacher recounts an example of her leadership in assessment redesign:

To encourage teachers' awareness of the problem with the language assessment scores, my colleague and I gave a professional development session in which we taught the staff the meaning of all of the terms used in language assessment and discussed the data for our school.

Roberta details "giving the teachers data" and taking them through a process of analysis, placement of students on a continuum of language development, and teaching them about the purposes of the assessment tool. "Since our staff is made up of very professional men and women who value student learning, we knew they would step up and do what it takes to help their students improve their scores." This team expressed some trepidation that their leadership might not be well received, but their commitment to the English learners at their school compelled them to take the risk. They were pleased to report higher test scores the following year.

Leadership Identity Development

The personal dimensions of leadership are visible every day to our students and colleagues, if not always to ourselves. We see the needs of our students and invite colleagues to support us in our advocacy. We recognize the importance of coaching our own children at home, and we struggle with the same dilemmas of balancing homework and downtime. Our practices are based on our suppositions about what parenting, teaching, and educational leadership are and can be. In our work setting, we make choices about the best use of our skills and interests. We notice places where we might fill a gap or lend a hand. Our colleagues recognize our gifts and ask for our consultation and support.

How we think about our work changes and evolves. We learn about ourselves in our work primarily as members of the community of the school. Striving to create communities of practice, we draw from many dimensions of leadership. This teacher considers the role of advocacy in leadership:

> I would definitely call myself a developing leader, because there are times when I don't feel comfortable standing up for what I believe is right, and there are definitely times when you have to step outside your comfort zone and advocate for something that is not wanted by the majority or the authority.

Hannah captures a central dilemma of leading—advocating for something that is unpopular versus standing with the minority because it is "right." So often leaders are expected to make ethical decisions on behalf of the least served, yet in schools even positional leaders may not believe they can challenge "the majority or the authority." In her next example, she recognizes a lack of expertise about district-level leadership by stating, "There are still areas within the school system that I need to learn about, such as the bus system and who determines who rides it." This is not a technical matter, but an instructional concern. Hannah recognizes there are district-level leaders who meet the compliance standard by assigning designated students to the right bus, but take no advocacy role to ensure that child was placed in the right program. Generally, the classroom teacher and the site specialist—not a centralized bureaucrat who may be handling dozens of cases—have the responsibility to advocate for individual students and to follow their stories as they unfold. It is ironic that classroom teachers who really know the students' needs consider central office work *real* leadership." Internalized views about management and leadership reside deep inside us. Images of managers as leaders are reflected back to us in myriad ways throughout the day. As my other colleagues do throughout this text, Hannah can define good leadership in relation to her own values and experiences:

> I do possess good leadership characteristics. I keep open lines of communication with my colleagues. I am honest and up-front. I am a good collaborator and becoming better each and every day. I regularly reflect on my practices. I have good relationships with my colleagues, and I make goals for myself and for my students. I do whatever it takes to make sure that the school does what is best for the students and community and that students feel successful.

Seeing Ourselves as Others See Us

A key factor in leadership socialization is recognition by our colleagues. Teachers who are committed learners will seek the expertise of peers to enhance their own practice. This kind of collaboration leads to improved learning for students. Positional leaders also seek out strong teachers to lead professional work in schools. A mid-career sixth-grade teacher related, "My principal asked me to take over as 'teacher of the day' when she is off-site. I guess that means I have the necessary skills to take over the school for a few hours." The understated tone of this remark suggests that this teacher wasn't told she had the skill set in so many words, yet she understood the informal recognition.

Professional socialization into formal or positional leadership presents a conundrum. The intertwined threads of the teacher-self contain skills of management, a philosophy of teaching and learning, and the ability to inspire others. But embracing formal roles of leadership can cause the threads to become tangled and knotty. For those who have been excluded from informal induction into leaderlike roles, such as women and people of color, recognition as a potential formal leader is a critical part of professional development. Most of us come to know ourselves as capable, smart teachers who can lead only when we recognize the work we do as leading.

Because the work of leading learning is deeply personal, our individual journeys are the nucleus of our practice. Taking time to revisit influential events is an important part of embracing personal dimensions of leadership within teaching. In our histories, we find people, places, and events that shaped our decisions and our beliefs about the purpose of schooling. The activities in the Inquiry section later in this chapter offer approaches to revisiting the roots of your leadership values and practices.

Assessing How Your Personal History Informs Your Leadership

Stepping Stones

- Know and respect your personal history as a leader.
- Draw upon your individual gifts and life events to inform your practice.

- Share your stepping stones or turning points with colleagues and students (without crossing the personal or professional line), so they can learn about different *ways* of learning, not simply *what* you learned.

In Loco Parentis (in the Place of Parents)

- Rethink your beliefs about the parallels and intersections between teaching and parenting. Be honest with yourself and others about the degree to which you draw from one role to inform the other.

- Recognize the benefits and limitations of "parenting" students the way you were parented or in ways that may reflect your culture, gender, or class. Be conscious about how and when you teach the whole child.

- Talk with parents about their hopes and aspirations for their children without imposing your own. Parents may want more formal education for their child, but not know how to support them in attaining that goal.

Gatekeeping

- Reconsider the gates that you have encountered and the roots of your beliefs about who can pass through those gates.

- Listen to your own thinking about access to education when you speak to students and parents. Are you providing honest information about how to negotiate gates, or are you perpetuating limitations—whether consciously or unconsciously—based on race, gender, or class?

- Recognize blatant and subtle gates that may be limiting your own professional development or your students' chances to move ahead. Form alliances with those who can open those gates for you, your colleagues, and your students.

✑ INQUIRY TWO ✑
Life Experiences Influence Your Practice

Following is a series of critical reflection activities that are useful for revisiting the personal experiences that influence your values as a teacher. The first, stepping stones, focuses on educational events in your own life that shaped your decision to become a teacher. The first part is a graphic organizer in which you can type or handwrite memories or events, and the second part contains prompts that invite you to make connections between those events and current practice.

Stepping Stones (Vocation)

Purpose: Identify your stepping stones as an educational leader.

There is a growing body of research on the ways our personal experiences as children and young adults shape professional choices, both the profession we choose and how we develop as adult learners. An important constructivist approach for adult learners is identifying turning points or making explicit for ourselves how early or recent experiences shape our beliefs and practices.

Stepping stones is a pedagogical approach taken from Progoff's (1992) *At a Journal Workshop*.[6] This simple yet powerful approach invites you to make connections between your current practice and past experience.

Complete the chart shown in Exhibit 2.1. Recall educational events from elementary, high school, undergraduate years,

Exhibit 2.1. Educational Experiences

	Event	Outcome	Decision(s) Made as a Result of That Experience
Elementary school years			
High school years			
College years			
Internship or job			

and early work settings that shaped your values as a learner and educator.

Critical reflection questions: Choose a stepping stone that was especially instructive in shaping your beliefs about educational leadership. Describe that experience in relation to the following:

1. How did your personal or cultural knowledge support you or limit your ability to make sense of what happened?

2. How did that experience shape your beliefs about teaching and learning?

3. How did that experience or other experiences influence your work as an educational leader?

Reflections on Teaching as Parenting (in Loco Parentis)

Purpose: Examine the ways parenting and teaching intersect, overlap, and conflict.

Read the vignette about Latino parents and their interactions with school staff on page 176 of Lisa Delpit's *Other People's Children.*[7] In that section, "Ignorance About Community Norms," Delpit describes how tensions can arise between teachers and parents. Briefly, teachers in an elementary school were frustrated by mothers who brought first graders into their classrooms before school. The mothers were concerned about a safe handoff, and the teachers were upset that their planning time was disrupted. Teachers locked their doors, and parents went to the school board.

In a small group, complete a T chart—a graphic organizer with a line down the center and two headings. Articulate the parent perspective on one side and the teacher perspective on the other side. Role-play the two sides. Discuss the role of the teacher in understanding parents, being a parent, and reconciling parents' expectations.

Identifying Gatekeepers (Profession)

Purpose: Learn about patterns of educational exclusion that arise through academic gatekeeping.

Gatekeeping is the process of academic tracking that funnels students into low, moderate, or more challenging classrooms and courses. Gatekeeping practices effectively limit student access to challenging curricula and prevent enrollment of some students in college-prep courses in high school. Gatekeeping reproduces inequity because minority and/or first-generation college-attending students often find themselves shut out of educational opportunities in secondary and post-secondary education.

1. Write a reflection on an experience or event from your elementary or secondary schooling in which you were excluded from an educational opportunity. What was the incident or event? When did you realize the implications for your academic career? What, if anything, did you or an advocate do about it? Do you see similar gatekeeping practices in your own school or district?

[*Activities 2 and 3 fit with Chapters Five and Six, on leading educational change at your district or in the larger community.*]

2. Using the resources listed at the end of this section, do some web-based research about civil rights concerns that have been raised at your school or another gatekeeping practice of which you are aware.

3. Choose an audience that will benefit from your research, including students, parents, colleagues, or central office administrators. Document your findings in a way that will be accessible and useful to your audience. Following are a few examples of accessible and useful findings:

Write a paragraph (seventy-five to a hundred words maximum) about why your colleagues should visit this web site, which articles they might read, and how staff, students, and community can benefit. Create a flyer using the text you've written and distribute it.

Create a poster or PowerPoint presentation in English and in the next most commonly spoken language at your school. Identify an event or meeting where your information would be well received. Identify a bilingual colleague (if needed) or community insider to copresent the information at a meeting or community gathering.

Write a letter to the editor, a blog, or another media outlet outlining your concerns and linking to web sites or other policy basics for end-users.

Web Resources

The Civil Rights Project
www.civilrightsproject.ucla.edu

EdSource Online
www.edsource.org

Ed Trust
www2.edtrust.org/edtrust

Learning Matters: John Merrow
www.pbs.org/merrow

Resources

Cameron, J., *The Artist's Way: A Spiritual Path to Higher Creativity*, 2nd ed. (New York: Jeremy Tarcher/Putnam, 2002).

This text acts as a self-discovery curriculum designed for a twelve-week course. Cameron is a writer and filmmaker, and she specializes in helping stuck artists get unstuck so they can more fully engage in their art or profession. There are examples, activities, and reflection strategies that serve anyone striving to improve herself.

Cattani, D. H., *A Classroom of Her Own: How New Teachers Develop Instructional, Professional, and Cultural Competence* (Thousand Oaks, Calif.: Corwin Press, 2002).

This text is a handbook for new teachers that pays particular attention to the professional induction experiences of young white women (who make up a high percentage of the teaching force). The researcher and her informants offer useful, step-by-step actions that can be taken during the stressful first years of teaching.

Center on School, Family, and Community Partnerships. www.csos.jhu.edu/p2000/center.htm

Joyce Epstein is known for her research and writing about schools, families, and community. This extensive web site has links to parent education information, articles, abstracts, and resources. The site also offers links to conferences and workshops for teachers, parents, and others seeking to build partnerships.

The Civil Rights Project at UCLA. www.civilrightsproject.ucla.edu

Formerly the Harvard Civil Rights Project, this organization offers rich resources for teachers and others seeking legal information about student and family civil rights. The links provide news, cases, legal developments, events, and other resources. The how-to dimension is under Resources: Community Tools and Legal Tools. Teachers have used this site and the research presented to change policies in their schools and districts.

Progoff, I., *At a Journal Workshop: Writing to Access the Power of the Unconscious and Evoke Creative Ability*, 2nd ed. (New York: Jeremy Tarcher/Putnam, 1992).

This large volume supports reflection about one's life journey, work, spirituality, and other dimensions of the self. The activities can be adapted to work settings such as schools, and the prompts and guidelines can be used by individuals or teams to explore personal histories as learners and teachers.

Schön, D. A., *Educating the Reflective Practitioner: How Professionals Think in Action* (New York: Basic Books, 1983).

Schön was a philosopher, a classically trained clarinetist, and an astute observer of how people make meaning from their work. His work on reflection-in-action draws from several professions and has informed the study of teaching as a profession and professionalism more generally. It's a complex piece and requires a commitment, but the time required to read it carefully is worth the investment.

Notes

The epigraph to this chapter is drawn from L. Delpit, *Other People's Children: Cultural Conflict in the Classroom* (New York: Norton, 1995).

1. National Commission on Teaching and America's Future, *What Matters Most: Teaching for America's Future* (Washington, D.C.: National Commission on Teaching and America's Future, 1996).

2. K. Casey, *I Answer with My Life: Life Histories of Women Teachers Working for Social Change* (New York: Routledge Press, 1993); M. Collay, "Recherche: Teaching Our Life Histories," *Teaching and Teacher Education* 14(3) (1998): 245–255; S. Nieto, *What Keeps Teachers Going?* (New York: Teachers College Press, 2003).

3. C. Gilligan, *In a Different Voice* (Boston: Harvard University Press); N. Noddings, *The Challenge to Care in Schools* (New York: Teachers College Press, 1992).

4. P. A. Noguera, "Preventing and Producing Violence: A Critical Analysis of Responses to School Violence," *Harvard Educational Review* 65(2) (1995): 189–212.

5. A. Etzioni, *The Semi-Professions and Their Organization: Teachers, Nurses, Social Workers*, ed. A. Etzioni (New York: Free Press, 1969); D. Lortie,

Schoolteacher (Chicago: University of Chicago Press, 1975); J. Gore and N. Morrison, "The Perpetuation of a (Semi-)Profession: Challenges in the Governance of Teacher Education," *Teaching and Teacher Education* 17 (2001): 567–582.

6. I. Progoff, *At a Journal Workshop: Writing to Access the Power of the Unconscious and Evoke Creative Ability* (New York: Jeremy P. Tarcher/ Putnam, 1992).

7. L. Delpit, *Other People's Children: Cultural Conflict in the Classroom* (New York: Norton, 1995).

3

TEACHING IS LEADING

To have an aim is to act with meaning.

—*John Dewey*

In every school, there are many teachers and one principal, with larger schools adding associates to the management team. Doing the math makes it clear that the majority of teachers do not become principals. The primary purpose of the school is teaching and learning, yet as a profession we continue to rank site leaders higher in status than classroom-based leaders. Teaching *is* leadership, and leadership begins in the classroom as teachers "act with meaning," seeking greater learning for their students and colleagues. Creating the conditions for learning is the work of people in schools. Instructional leadership happens every day, all day. In this chapter, I position the classroom as the nucleus of leadership in schools. Instructional design, implementation, and assessment practices emanate from that essential core.

The integrity required for good teaching compels teachers to go beyond the four walls of the classroom to ensure students can learn. Within this chapter and the next two, my colleagues and I discuss leading in the classroom, the kinds of collaboration required to prepare, plan, and sustain instruction, and forms of inquiry teachers use to strengthen practice. Teaching, collaboration, and inquiry are organizing concepts for the next three chapters as these big ideas intersect and flow into each other. I also address leadership in the classroom, school, district, and community throughout these chapters. While different teachers choose different actions at different times, these three levels of activity are integral to the work of leading in schools.

The classroom is perceived as a box with four walls, rather than the nucleus of a cell. The box metaphor is limiting, constructed with four walls that limit possibilities of who and what can pass in and out, and leads to adages like "closing one's door" to minimize outside distraction or avoid predictable distractions. A more vital image is the classroom as a cell, a rich center with a permeable membrane, capable of guiding teaching and learning. This second image may not immediately come to mind because we have spent a lifetime in box-shaped classrooms, and our learning experiences in real life often happen outside them. As teachers work with the gifts and challenges students present, most feel a moral imperative to push through the walls that limit learning to create some form of osmosis, streams of connection that pass both directions. The metaphor of the cell offers a dynamic alternative: a sustainable model of codified information, channels for interaction, and great potential to develop the many beings within the school.

Once the classroom is reconsidered as a developmentally engaging place for learning to occur, the teacher as leader of that learning has a much more expansive and facilitative role. Reframing teaching as leadership is the primary purpose of this chapter. As you read, think about the metaphors you hear and the language you use to describe teaching and learning in classrooms, schools, or beyond. Then reexamine your own beliefs about what teaching is and can be.

Reframing Teaching as Leadership

If we agree that teaching is both a calling and a profession, then some who are called to work directly with children and young people may not interested in "moving up," as might occur in other lines of work. In educational settings, choosing or being asked to manage adults and systems requires moving away from the core enterprise. It means reduced contact with students, separation from the moral purpose of teaching, and less direct influence on and satisfaction from classroom-centered work. Teachers who have a knack for management and can keep the trains running on time may shy away from the perceived stress, focus on personnel management, and politicized dynamics of the site leadership role. The shift from classroom-centered leadership to school oversight is most challenging, however, because of the nature of schools as organizations. Most schools are part of large, complex districts, and school principals are middle managers. Some progressive schools or those less bound by union structures designate a head teacher or a colleague who has agreed to manage the organization for a period of time. Rotating leadership is more common at other levels of the organization, as with the roles of department chair, team leader, or project leader. However, the principalship as it has evolved is highly bureaucratic and political, with accountability concerns and gatekeeping prominent features of the work. Few teachers regard the principal as an instructional leader, even if their colleague has curricular expertise. The role is not currently designed for principals to fully engage with colleagues around teaching and learning.

Following are some of the factors that influence decision making about shifting leadership activities from instructional work with students and colleagues to school management.

- *Societal expectations.* Most teachers do not become principals, but more often choose other forms of leadership. Historically, women chose teaching when few other professions were open to them, partly because of the work calendar and partly because women were not seen as fit to manage other adults. Some research on school leadership and gendered role expectations considers parenting a primary "limitation" that prevents women from seeking positional leadership. The long days and longer school-year work patterns still hinder some women from accepting administrative roles, especially those with heavy family responsibilities for child care or elder care. We can reframe this "work is life" metaphor, however, by looking at work-life balance research. Rather than characterizing teaching as women's work and noting that most women teachers choose *not* to become principals, we can reframe the decision to work directly with students as a commitment to instructional leadership.

- *Limited opportunities to learn about site leadership.* The structure of the school places one teacher with a group of students and separates adults from each other. The "egg-carton" structure of schools limits collegial professional development, since each teacher is cloistered in a classroom with twenty to forty students and has few adult interactions throughout the day. Neither peer leadership nor positional leadership is visible from the classroom, and learning opportunities with other adults must be sought out.

- *Relationships with colleagues.* Teachers who take on management and oversight tasks usually carried out by the principal may be perceived as "going to the dark side," leaving the student-centered work of the classroom for a more distant, less intimate role. More commonly, experienced teachers are called upon to mentor and support new teachers and to share disciplinary expertise with others. This form of collaboration is highly valued by the givers and the receivers with few exceptions. Peer collaboration on behalf of students is fully accepted as part of the work of teaching, while stepping away from a classroom focus is sometimes perceived as defection from the moral purpose of education.

- *Relationships with students.* There are women and men who are able and willing to take positional leadership and still find the work less fulfilling than teaching. Teachers who display organizational skills and are identified as potential managers may articulate a preference to stay closer to the client and further from the "adult issues," which are the often less-satisfying managerial requirements of the contemporary principal. These include a focus on bureaucratic compliance, constant search for resources, lack of authority to hire and fire, union concerns, high percentages of undereducated students, disgruntled parents, and relatively low pay.

- *Patterns of gender, race, and class of positional leaders.* Historically, school leaders identify those who look like themselves and hold similar values to mentor, which reproduces a limited pool of aspiring principals. Women and people of color will often be overlooked in the informal mentoring process, even if they are as skilled and experienced as a white male. Such exclusionary practices are changing in urban districts, but do persist and remain common in other settings.

This list of concerns identified by various researchers may not tell the whole story. What if teachers find their greatest efficacy in working directly with children and young people? What if school leadership were classroom-centered, and administrators who supported classroom instruction from outside the classroom were considered support staff? This perspective reframes how we perceive the work of teaching as a powerful act of leadership, a stance seldom considered in the literature. One exception is the work on "servant-leadership" similar to transformative leadership. Both types of leadership emphasize vision, trust, modeling, consideration of others, empowering others, and communication.[1] Stone and colleagues suggest that "transformational leaders tend to focus more on organizational objectives while servant leaders focus more on the people who are their followers." Another approach to reframing leadership for transformative schooling by teachers and principals together is described by Crowther, Fergusson, and Hann as "parallel leadership."[2] Implications for school leaders include an important focus on supporting teachers through strong relationships. Teachers have many peers with whom to build relationships, unlike principals who may feel alone at the site and are designated to oversee others. Relationship building between "supervisors" and "workers" is not generally accepted practice, another vestige of the management-staff hierarchy.

Choosing Classroom Leadership over School Site Management

Positional leadership in schools requires formal training and an additional credential that is different from a teaching credential. The principal's credential requires coursework and a supervised internship, which means teachers who aspire to the principal-ship must enroll in graduate coursework and have opportunities to undertake principal-type tasks. Professional socialization into the management role begins before individuals apply to a credential program, although without great depth. Teachers see many dimensions of peer leadership throughout the day and principal leadership more sporadically. Therefore, their understanding of what it means to lead as a teacher is deeper and more developed. Many teachers considering other forms of school leadership describe a moral imperative in their decision to remain in the classroom. The classroom is a space and place for professional expression. As one teacher states, "Caring about my students and working for their success is something that comes naturally."

Teachers know less about what principals do, as images of schoolwide leadership are less powerfully shaped by the childhood apprenticeship of sitting in classrooms. Few adults who aren't directly involved with schools know what principals do. Teachers learn about building-level leadership as they move beyond the early years' socialization pattern into the mid-career ranks of experience. Teachers learn that most principals are white, that most secondary school principals are male, and that many relinquish physical, mental, and psychic health to do the job. If teachers are truly dedicated to the vocation of working with young people, moving away from direct contact with students may prove untenable.

Some teachers qualify for a principal credential program, but choose a teacher leadership focus instead. In their applications for a master's degree program they responded to this prompt: "Why are you interested in participating in the teacher leadership master's degree program at this time?" Andrea, a Latina female elementary teacher wrote: "I would like to become a leader and role model for my students. . . . I myself have had to deal with social injustices, and I feel this program will equip me with strategies to help all students succeed and feel confident about their educational endeavors."

In this next response, Mona, an African American special education teacher, makes a connection between her experience as a person of color and her students' experiences in school: "Successful teachers of students of color acknowledge the realities that students encounter and work with them to increase equity and opportunity." Iris, another African American middle school teacher, makes a similar claim: "I believe that our kids are being misrepresented, and their needs are not being met." Like Mona, Iris believes "there is a need for minorities in and out of the classroom to insure that our students receive the best quality of education there is." Early in her teaching career Iris was standing in as "principal for the day" while her principal was offsite. A white female high school teacher declared: "Urban education is in dire need of repair by dedicated individuals if we are indeed to prepare our youth to be successful in a world filled with inequity and discrimination." This teacher was also very active on her small school's leadership team, taking on many of the responsibilities of a site administrator.

Each of these applicants met the requirements for the principal credential program. All were women in their late twenties and early thirties. One of the four is a parent of a young child. Their reasons for electing teacher leadership primarily had to do with their perceptions of the role of principal as less satisfying and their own self-concept that they were not "principal material." Their gender, race, and social class may have played a role in their rationale for staying close to the client. They may not have benefited from sponsorship by their principals or may have indicated lack of interest in positional leadership. Once teachers undertake formal study of school leadership, however, some who resisted site leadership roles change their stance, while others who saw themselves as aspiring principals decide they prefer classroom-based leadership.

On average, 41 percent of teachers have fewer than nine years of experience before seeking the principalship, and 59 percent of teachers have ten years or more experience.[3] A staff of experienced teachers will include a handful of individuals who have earned the principal credential and continue to lead from the classroom. Many experienced teachers participate in discipline-based professional organizations, regional organizations that support teacher professional development, and formal partnerships with nonprofit organizations such as the Coalition of Essential Schools or the National Writing Project. These leadership settings and activities are discussed in Chapter Six.

Perceiving Oneself as a Leader

Beliefs about differences between the roles and responsibilities of principals and teachers run deep. This section presents common perceptions that are may be unexamined yet become taken-for-granted. One is the assumption that teachers work with students, and principals work with adult staff at the site and beyond. Experienced teachers lead within and across settings, but their main focus is their own classroom. Sometimes implied but more often explicit is the belief that leading colleagues challenges the egalitarian norms of membership in a corps. Teachers report tension between colleagues or with supervisors because stepping out of the classroom disrupts the status quo.[4] Other research addresses the tension many teachers feel about choosing or accepting administrative roles.[5] Following are some voices of leaders reflecting on their beliefs about leading.

An early years' Latina teacher reflected on her earlier thinking about "becoming" a leader: "To begin with, I never saw myself as a leader, I always thought of myself as a follower." Embedded in her words is the assumption that there are leaders and followers, and perhaps teachers are followers. Indeed, much of the literature about leadership addresses the requirement for leaders to have followers.

Beliefs about who can lead are portrayed through versions of trait theory—that is, certain people have "what it takes" to be a leader. I have heard: "My colleague has the traits or characteristics to lead adults, I do not." This belief is grounded in real-world participant observation. All adults have twelve years of school-based observations of the individuals who serve as principals, and teachers have spent additional years observing principals from the role of teacher. Teachers of color do not often see people like themselves in the principal's office.

Another influence on role perception is social class. Many teachers are the first in their families to be college-educated. Those first-generation college-educated individuals who come back into schools as credentialed teachers are already a giant step beyond their parents and other family members with regard to formal education. The idea that they could also become "the boss" may be a cultural reach for them. Andrea emigrated from Mexico to the United States as a child and began her career as a social worker: "I always felt that a leader was someone in an administrative role or who worked at the district level. But now that I have gained more knowledge as to how one can lead within and outside of the classroom as an educator, I am more willing to pursue additional responsibilities aside from those I hold as a teacher that might help my site build a more collaborative and inquisitive community."

Andrea initially saw leadership as work outside the classroom, but now recognizes leadership occurs "within and outside" of it. Again, many teachers have internalized images of leading as management, rather than recognizing that leading in schools is supporting learning of young people and colleagues.

The prevalence of society-wide assumptions about the "hero-leader" does not diminish our strong instincts that "real" leadership is collaborative and democratic. Niko, a thirty-five-year-old biracial elementary teacher with extensive urban credentials, captures the essence of school leadership as relationship-based, rather than role-centered: "Although many individuals may be motivated or interested in roles and/or positions of leadership, it's more challenging and critical to understand, respect, and appreciate the team and community dynamics that absolutely demand establishing meaningful relationships and rely on the cooperation and joint work of its members."

Niko values his ability to work well across roles and responsibilities at his school, even has he recognizes the complexity of those relationships. Susan, an African American elementary teacher, offers a similar perspective about the importance of relationships between adults that supports a commitment to student learning: "*Leadership*—now that's a frequently used word in the field of education. When I hear the word *leadership*, I actually think of someone who carries out the ideas of others, a 'behind-the-scenes' visionary. A 'leader' is a coach. An effective coach is a good communicator and listener. This type of leader is disciplined and consistent; they lead by example and are committed to their colleagues and students."

Susan attributes leadership capacity to a broad spectrum of individuals in the tradition of distributed leadership. She still acknowledges "the system's" power and authority over teachers. "There are many leaders within a school community: the administrator, the teachers, the support staff, the students, the parents, and the community working collaboratively, collectively, and constructively as a whole. It used to be that the principal was the leader of all the teachers, and they were to follow what he or she said without question. Fortunately, the educational system has evolved in letting teachers utilize their skills and talents by becoming leaders within the school."

This last point demonstrates how far teachers have yet to travel on the road to professional status. Even though Susan states a strong value for "collaborative, collective, and constructive" leadership and acknowledges teacher expertise, she retains the notion that "the system *lets* teachers utilize skills and talents." The same thought also contains the seeds of school leadership as Susan articulates an essential dimension of teacher leadership—skills and talent.

Creating Better Conditions for Learning

Rethinking school leadership requires us to reconsider authority in schools. We know from our own practice and research that classroom instruction is the most important factor influencing student achievement. Teachers spend time with students and are the holders of expertise about content and how students learn. Yet we continue to place greater authority in the positional leader, usually the principal. Leithwood, Jantzi, and Steinbach[6] offer this helpful perspective: "In a traditional school, for example, those in formal administrative roles have greater access than teachers to positional power in their attempts to influence practice, whereas teachers may have greater access to the power that flows from technical expertise."

Teachers attribute their own learning to peers in most cases, rather than the principal or professional developers who are not regular members of the staff. They vest authority in their own experience and in their colleagues' technical expertise. Many teachers are committed to developing their own curriculum and testing their ideas before carrying them forward.

In addition to content expertise, educational leaders must have a values-centered stance about the work of teaching and learning. The characteristics of an educational leader outlined by Mendez-Morse include "believing that schools are for learning."[7] This point may seem obvious, yet current reform mandates require a "highly qualified teacher" in every classroom, indicating that there are qualitative differences between teachers and that not all classrooms contain such a person. "Highly qualified" should mean more than a person with the right credential. It should also mean teachers who will hold learners to a high standard. Poorly prepared teachers, early years' teachers, and those who have chosen the wrong line of work are not as competent as more experienced, committed teachers. Teachers who have good classroom management, strong content knowledge, and critical pedagogical skills to reach their students have the greatest influence on student learning. Skills are required, but they are not sufficient. Leading in the classroom requires teachers to hold high expectations of students.[8] This powerful combination of skill and stance is the foundation of educational leadership. Hallinger compares instructional leadership that focuses on creating conditions for learning with transformation leadership that affects how the capacity of the organization is strengthened.[9] Both approaches to change depend on teachers.

Creating better conditions for student learning means creating similar conditions for colleagues. The tradition of bringing outside experts to "in-service" teachers has created a nonprofessional terrain that is hard to reshape. Taking responsibility to support colleagues' professional development requires a breadth of leadership abilities, but more than that, it requires a belief that teachers themselves hold the knowledge needed to lead transformation of education. Catching and holding a different understanding of "communities of practice" requires a different metaphor for the place of knowledge in teaching and learning.

Leading Learning in the Classroom and Beyond

The image of the cell, with DNA in the nucleus at the center, is a vital metaphor that allows us to think differently about teaching and learning in the classroom. When contained in a box, the teaching and learning enterprise is portrayed as static, dependent upon canned materials, and limited by the space. When portrayed as the nucleus of a cell, the enterprise gains a blueprint, interactions, osmosis (exchanges), and growth. The cell is also part of a living organism. If the information in the nucleus informs the larger body, the nucleus is of greatest value to the development of the larger organism. The cell is served by nutrients and other activity occurring outside, but it has the essential information within it. Compare this image to the box with its fixed walls and sometimes closed door. With open, active osmosis in mind, consider the following actions that teachers initiate within their classrooms and beyond.

Leading with Professional Expertise

Teachers bring a lifetime of personal and professional experience to the classroom, all of which informs teaching practice. Our socialization in the larger society shapes our beliefs about classroom-based leadership and positional leadership, in particular the idea that teaching isn't leadership. I believe that leadership is a moral and ethical enterprise encompassing the characteristics outlined by Mendez-Morse in Chapter One: vision, beliefs, valuing human resources, good communication, proactivity, and taking risks.[10] Powerful leadership is that which most influences the lives of students, and higher leadership status should not be automatically conferred on those further from the classroom. Once we embrace the notion that teaching is leadership, we don't need to dichotomize classroom-based leadership and site-based leadership. Much can be learned about how school leadership functions by looking at teacher practice in collaboration with students and colleagues. Within the daily, weekly, monthly, and annual calendar of collaboration about teaching and learning are powerful forms of leadership.

Educational leadership resides in teacher expertise. What teachers know about how children learn is expressed to a great degree in the classroom, and that knowledge is informed by forces within and beyond the school. What effective teachers know is how to create the conditions for learning. *Instruction* has multiple meanings, but the more common one is "imparting information," rather than the less common one, "the act or practice of instructing or teaching." "Teaching and learning" is a bit clumsy, and doesn't trip easily off the tongue. Doing it well isn't easy, either, but I'll continue to use these terms together. Leadership for learning is also complex in word and deed. While it includes the work of instruction, it is much, much more.

Unlike some professions, improving one's practice as a teacher is hindered by the isolation of the classroom, something akin to each school being like an egg carton and each classroom a separate container. Individual teachers work with groups of children or young people, having few opportunities for teaming or side-by-side work with others. Rarely do teachers see their colleagues in the act of teaching. While in the laboratory of their own classrooms, they have regular opportunities to test ideas and refine them, but few opportunities to receive feedback on practice. Teachers learn to teach reading or science or to structure classroom management by trial and error and, if they're fortunate, by gleaning second-hand information from generous colleagues. The adage, "we teach as we were taught" is a truism, as each of us undergoes an apprenticeship of sixteen or more years of teacher observation.[11] Even with the limitations described above, leaders find ways to improve their teaching on the job, reframing that apprenticeship of childhood experience through regular reflection, experimentation, and application.

Leading Through Student Advocacy

Teachers, like any group of professionals, come in all shapes and sizes and with a variety of professional and personal experiences that inform their practice. For example, on a team of five first-grade teachers there might be individuals with liberal studies, history, math, or science degrees. They might be mid-career changers from banking, management, or marketing; they might range in age from twenty-five to sixty-five years old; and they may be parents or grandparents. They may have formal training as emergency medical technicians, firefighters, engineers, forest rangers, or in the fine arts. Their hobbies might include Friends of the Earth, scout leadership, sports coaching, or backpacking. Leaders with wide-ranging skills return to schools as fully developed adults and enter a flat organization where leadership is practiced for the most part in the company of children and young people. Many teachers also serve as mentors and coaches of young people outside the classroom. People who like leading learning tend to take similar leadership roles in settings beyond the school.

Tom became a teacher in his late forties after an earlier career in nursing: "I have a twenty-year record of working in medical research and health care." He describes his own educational journey with conflicting thoughts: "I have argued and written papers in support of bilingual education and affirmative action. I do not know if my experience as an English language learner influenced my decision to become a leader for equity." My own research suggests Tom's life experience had a profound effect on his values and advocacy. He describes his commitment to advocacy for students: "Improving my subject-matter expertise and instruction in math has been high on my list of priorities. I have chosen to specialize in teaching mathematics in middle school rather than teach elementary school because math at this level is a 'gatekeeper' for minority students."

Tom is a mature leader with a deep interest in making education accessible to students who have been excluded. Math in middle school is not just another subject among many: math is a make-or-break discipline that prevents many minority (and some majority) students from gaining access to college prep courses in high school. Tom's choice to teach middle school is an act of advocacy leadership, as he uses his math knowledge, language skills, and cultural understanding to bring more students through the middle school math sequence prepared for high school.

Leading Through Mentoring

While teachers come into the classroom with some or lots of leadership experience, classroom-based leadership is refined through peer support. At the site, informal teams share instructional practices and curriculum designs and strive to improve their assessments. In those discussions, teacher lore is also shared, including stress management, work-life balance strategies, and the endless tricks of the trade that teachers use to sustain themselves and their work.

The egg carton metaphor depicts an image of professional isolation of teachers from colleagues who do the same work and from positional leaders. The nature of classroom teaching limits teachers' access to mentoring by both roles. While the structure of school limits opportunities for classroom teachers to learn more about what positional leaders actually do, teachers lead every day. Individuals within a school are clustered by role and by the students they serve, and have few opportunities to work side by side with a positional leader. How do competent teachers lead throughout all aspects of the teaching and learning enterprise? Professional development for leadership occurs in a parallel process with learning about instruction in grade- or department-level teams, site-based informal working groups, site- or district-based formal instruction, and independently sought or recommended "training opportunities" outside the school or district.

Teachers, like any group of professionals, bring varying amounts of expertise and learn the craft after taking their first teaching position. Most consider an apprenticeship of three to five years essential for development into an experienced teacher. Because half of all teachers who enter the profession do not stay in the classroom beyond five years, the number of newcomers each year remains steady. Principals and experienced teachers understand the challenges of early years' teaching and, in most cases, work proactively to support their newest colleagues. "To teach is to learn twice over," and those who extend a helping hand to the newest members move from informal helping to more formal mentoring programs offered in some districts. They themselves become more expert, and at some point other colleagues refer the newest teachers to those most likely to mentor or who have specific expertise. Their work is then recognized more formally and they gain authority for their peer leadership. Susan describes her stance as a mentor in this way:

> When new teachers come into my school, I know that they will be overwhelmed with a lot of different paperwork, regulations, and policies in addition to daily classroom teaching. I have offered my advice and help to teachers whenever they have asked and sometimes when they have not. I give them advice instead of telling them what they need to do. I use the examples of my failures to help them understand what they need to do. I have always had an open-door policy in my classroom. People have learned that they can come to me for anything. If I don't have the answer, I will help them get the answer.

In most situations, teachers have benefited from helpful mentors and will repay the favor by continuing to work informally as mentors. Peer support can include inducting the newest member of the team by sharing materials and resources, turn-teaching in one's stronger suit so the newcomer has fewer preparations, keeping the most challenging students instead of loading up the newcomer with the discipline problems, and offering moral support. As Susan points out, colleagues seek out the experts among them when they need to solve problems or learn new things. This mentor acts as an instructional leader every day by keeping her door open.

Leading Through Curriculum Design

Once in the classroom, teachers ask questions about how students learn, about the materials they are provided, about the ways students experience school, and about how student learning is measured. Most teacher inquiry begins with curriculum and instruction. Teachers are prepared to lead others, but only after a thorough test in the laboratory of their classrooms. Mary outlines her thinking here: "If I take these six students and work them through the writing process focusing on an important person in American history, I can use what I have learned to implement the curriculum in a whole-group setting. Once I have implemented it successfully in my own classroom, then perhaps I can present it to my grade level or upper-grade circuits. This might very well be the beginning of a curriculum that is needed about the different Americans that live in our community and what makes them special and unique—it never hurts to dream big."

Mary characterizes sharing practice about the teaching of writing as "dreaming big." Mary's pursuit of her big dream is an act of leadership. Imagine another profession where testing approaches to the work and inviting others to consider your ideas is such a stretch. Teachers may be shy about advocating for poorly performing students among colleagues who do not share their enthusiasm. The current national reform agenda of high-stakes testing and punishment of those in failing schools gives teachers good reason to distance themselves from the lowest-performing students. Thankfully, many stay in the work despite the culture of castigation.

Teachers make long-term curriculum plans and shorter-term implementation plans. Teachers assess what students know and figure out alternative approaches to learning for those students who don't succeed. Teachers grapple with the next new version of state-adopted textbooks and adapt those materials to what they know actually works. Curriculum design is a powerful form of educational leadership. This excerpt shows a philosopher of education at work: "With my kindergarteners I have attempted to implement Freire-influenced learning by supporting student independence and leadership, as well as allowing students opportunities to create knowledge together and ask each other questions instead of only answering the teacher's questions." Lisa is not imparting information, but rather developing human beings who can create their own learning. She has aspirations for her students that include self-direction and autonomy. "They are really little, but they are asking each other, 'Why do we learn letters?' Their answers are very illustrative and include, 'Because the teacher is showing us. So that we can count. Because we need to learn them.'"

Lisa described her own and her students' philosophy of why they want to learn. Her description of creating conditions for learning through dialogue reflects Freire's practices and demonstrates her belief that "schools are for learning" and that learning should be emancipatory.

Teachers share knowledge about curriculum informally through everyday conversation, sharing resources and materials, and problem-solving in the hallway. Teachers recognize the value of their colleagues' expertise in supporting each other's instruction, but don't always characterize that expertise as leadership. If the purpose of schooling is teaching and learning, then what can be more powerful leadership than sharing instructional practice? Curriculum development occurs primarily in horizontal teams, where those who teach the same age or the same content work together to design and implement curriculum and evaluate its effect on student learning. Everett offers a good example of colleagues using a cycle of inquiry to refine their practice: "I have examined academic standards and reflected upon curricular ideas with my grade-level team. Our team now meets weekly to focus on continuous improvement in our teaching and learning. I encourage my team to make learning more collaborative and democratic by modeling a variety of content and language-based activities in our classrooms. Through rubrics, scaffolding, collaborative activities, and reflection, we try to make content learning more accessible to all students."

Such inquiry work is as relevant and powerful with students in the classroom as it is for professional development. This teacher makes direct connections between the work he does with his grade-level team and leadership: "My grade-level cohort now models and facilitates the same cycle of inquiry and continuous improvement with our students that we use for ourselves." The weekly meetings formalize the co-construction of new knowledge that was probably occurring informally. Combining interest and expertise in one's own instruction with a commitment to sharing practice more publicly moves private practice into the open air of public practice. Greater expertise also positions teachers to lead curriculum development and instructional practice across grade levels or disciplines.

Leading Professional Development

After leading grade-level or discipline-centered curriculum development, the next level of work often requires the full staff's engagement. Smaller teams who have worked through modifications within the smaller unit are well positioned to lead change on a larger scale. In this next example, two teachers with an interest in improving assessment of English language learners took their project to teachers of other grades.

"To encourage teachers' awareness of the problem with English language assessment, Fran and I offered a professional development session at a staff meeting. We taught the staff the meaning of all of the terms used in language assessment and discussed the data for our school." Roberta described how they walked their colleagues through a student-by-student evaluation protocol. "It was a powerful visual representation that showed teachers that most of our students were clustered at level three.

We then explained what skills were required for a student to advance beyond level three." Roberta shows confidence in her leadership and the potential leadership of her colleagues: "Since our staff is made up of very professional men and women who value student learning, we knew they would rise to the occasion and step up and do what it takes to help their students improve their scores."

Teachers have expertise in one or more content areas as well as skills in classroom management, technology, or assessment strategies. Teachers with more general elementary education degrees often have baccalaureate degrees in a major discipline. Teachers also learn on the job about the topics they teach, including content knowledge and how best to teach that content in that setting. Many elementary teachers and all secondary teachers have one or more areas of content specialization, and these areas become part of their identity. They are often called upon to share their content and pedagogy expertise with new teachers, grade-level teams, or departments.

At the secondary level, the majority of peer support and informal mentoring happens within the department, as teachers plan curriculum, instructional strategies, and assessment. Colleagues with similar roles develop curriculum and instructional approaches together and may turn-teach or develop specialization within their discipline. In smaller schools or for project-based activity, teachers may work on interdisciplinary teams and develop their instructional identity as the "fine arts person" or the "science person" in relation to that team. These identities are borne out by acts of instructional leadership: teachers judge art shows, conduct musicals, and set up science fairs as part of their instruction, thus becoming more visible as leaders to other teachers, parents, and administrators. They also model leadership actions for young people. Teachers lead by developing their own disciplinary expertise and creating the conditions where others can learn.

Reimagining Instructional Leadership

Some contend that much of what makes a teacher a leader requires inhabiting roles and actions that reflect what positional leaders do. Yet the modern principalship has evolved away from focus on the classroom, and bureaucratic demands force principals to distribute responsibility for learning. The work of leading learning should be the focal point of every school staff member, whether paraprofessional, teacher, specialist, or site leader. While much research on educational reform exhorts the principal to be an instructional leader, the expertise to lead instruction lies in the teacher ranks. Those doing the instruction are not always seen as leaders in their own right, but they are charged with the task of creating conditions for learning and already lead this work. If instructing students were deemed a fully professional act, acts of leadership in that domain would be fully acknowledged. Recall that teachers are considered "semiprofessionals" to be managed by principals and central office administrators. How many times have we said or heard someone say, "I'm just a teacher"? You won't hear "I'm just a lawyer," not the owner of the firm, or "I'm just a doctor," not in charge of the hospital. These professionals have authority, make decisions about the content and scope of work, and have more control over their professional circumstances. Professionals do not include management and staff metaphors in their language, and they do not describe a supervisor "letting" them take leadership or make decisions. It is imperative, therefore, that teachers have multiple opportunities to transform "just teaching" into "teaching as leadership." Teachers and others can reframe their work as professional, somewhat autonomous, and requiring leadership skills, rather than internalizing a set of semiprofessional values that hold separate the title of "leader" for principals. Placing instruction at the center of educational leadership will contribute to the reimagining of what teachers know and do as leadership. Recall the metaphor of the cell as a living organism that contains everything needed to grow the organism.

One powerful way to recognize instructional expertise and strengthen a community of practice is through regular, systematic inquiry about student learning. Many good models and protocols are available, so there is no need to reinvent the wheel. They can be found under the umbrella of professional learning communities, child study, teacher-led inquiry, action research guidelines, or protocols from organizations such as the Coalition of Essential Schools, the National Equity Project, or the National School Reform Faculty. These are readily accessible online. Processes for evaluating student work also reside in organizations that support specific content area development (see Chapter Six). As a professional development coach, I always encourage staff members or small teams of teachers to find a review process that supports their team's goals and can be aligned with school or district goals. Minutes for collaboration are dear and should be used as much as possible for applied work. Modifying protocols and revising prompts, standards, and formats can be time-consuming and unproductive. What matters is the opportunity to engage in systematic, collaborative ways with questions about student learning.

In addition to web sites, there are many books and articles that contain strategies to support personal and professional reflection through prompts, readings, questionnaires, and other "third things." Many professional development programs for teachers and other leaders use such strategies to engage individuals and groups in examining their values, beliefs, and practices as teachers, teacher leaders, and positional leaders. Instructional leadership is the lifeblood of the school, and leading instruction transformation requires a clear vision, a strong belief in students as learners, and well-developed content knowledge. Good communication, a commitment to sharing resources, and expertise in adult development will move student-centered leadership outward from the classroom and create the conditions for a larger scope of influence. Draw upon the expertise in your school and the professional development staff in your district, county office of education, nonprofit agency, or other partners for resources and models. Ask a colleague to share her discipline-based materials with you and your students or come into your classroom and model her favorite classroom management strategies. You might be surprised at what you learn! Offer your expertise to others when asked. Brokering expertise is a skill that must be practiced to create a community of practice.

Considerations About Teaching as Leading

- Reframe teaching as leadership by recognizing all leadership actions that support teaching and learning.
- Teach young people and colleagues with the same commitment to the learning of both these groups.
- Identify systemic influences that support and disrupt conditions for learning.
- Design, implement, and evaluate curriculum: this work is central to educational leadership.
- Attend to the intellectual, emotional, and physical development of the student through authentic student assessment. Authentic assessment is an art and a science that is most powerful in the hands of professionals.
- All students learn differently, and all students can learn together.

✐ INQUIRY THREE ✐
Student and Curriculum Case Studies

Following are two approaches to teacher-led inquiry that create a relevant framework for instructional transformation. Case studies draw out individual teacher expertise and strengthen professional development. The case of student or curriculum is served, and information gleaned from the case benefits other students, teachers and the program. In the first example, the student is the focus of inquiry, and in the second, a unit of curriculum is the focus of inquiry.

Student Case Study

A formal or informal student case study can be done by any teacher any time, or by a group of teachers collaborating to understand how individual students are engaging with a unit of study or school in general. This approach is student-centered, rather than curriculum-centered, and supports more formal documentation of the observations teachers make every day. A careful look at one student, however, informs teachers about how most students are engaging with the material. Student case studies are especially helpful when one or a few students are struggling with specific content. Teachers often have knowledge of student background and learning history, but don't have time and support to document that information. The decision to document a case creates an opportunity to look carefully at one situation with the prospect that a closer look will inform one's practice more generally.

Choose a student whose work can inform your inquiry question. In the current climate of "data-driven instruction," teachers sometimes choose "focus students"—a few students who represent certain characteristics or levels of achievement. For example, if your team, grade level, or department is implementing a unit of instruction, you can choose three focus students who perform at the lowest, middle, and highest quintile on standardized assessments. As you take the whole class through each part of the unit, you already capture, review, and analyze the learning demonstrated by all students. For those three students, however, you will take a second or third look at their materials in a more focused way.

Another example involves choosing a student who is unsuccessful in one subject area, then creating a more comprehensive record of that student's evaluations. The student case can be framed as one student in one subject for one term or unit. A third example is following a high-performing student or students through the academic unit, term, or year, refining a set of assessments that become the basis of an inquiry about how students learn in your classroom over time. Use that information to evaluate both the student's development and the learning setting.

Creating simple case studies for many students would be too time-consuming for most settings, but a few cases can provide great insight. Do it for one assignment or one unit of instruction. Consider having students in one class or in one subject area create a portfolio of their work over time so they can assess themselves using their own materials. Invite colleagues to gather similar student work, so that you can all use it to ground your collaboration time. Always treat students equitably and ethically, taking their materials to colleagues with great care and confidentiality. Following is an outline that might be helpful.

Describe the Student   Who is the student? If it's helpful, you can break the question down into these three parts:

1. Academic dimensions
2. Social-emotional dimensions
3. Developmental dimensions

Document Yearlong Assessment Data   Assemble samples of the student's work, including writing, artwork, sloppy copy or final copy, math worksheets, or science notes from a single project. This material can serve as a "pretest" that you and the student can use to compare with end-of-year work later on.

Collect Diagnostic Information and Project Short- and Long-Term Outcomes   After you assemble the case (description and general assessments), you can choose an additional diagnostic tool or tools that will help you support the student's learning between now and the end of May. Use online or reference-based ideas, tools, and strategies, talk to your colleagues, and set a timeline. Remember: you can give the whole class the assessment and look more carefully at your case study student. You don't necessarily need to pull the student out at recess for a special evaluation.

Set Student Learning Goals for the Balance of the Year   Student learning goals should be very specific and measurable. For instance, if the student is achieving below the standard in reading, you might set meeting the standard as a goal, even though you won't know the results until after the year is over. In addition, set local and measurable goals—weekly tests, vocabulary usage, the final writing assessment, chapter tests, test prep materials answers. You can set a goal within the larger assessment, such as "learn times tables up to 12" or "meet or exceed state standard on vocabulary development."

You can use the same categories cited previously for these goals:

1. Academic dimensions (reading, writing, and math)

2. Social-emotional dimensions (a behavioral goal)

3. Developmental dimensions (you can't force maturation, but you can track it!)

Identify References That Inform Your Case   You can use print materials from your own library, your school, district, or local library and online references. For instance, writing assessments are generally adopted by the school or district. Use the descriptions with students and colleagues to standardize expectations and feedback.

Offer examples of articles that inform your case. For instance, you are unsure whether a child is caught between first- and second-language acquisition and delayed in both or might actually have a learning disability. Standardized assessments don't reveal the information you need. You can use literature that addresses second-language acquisition, early detection of reading problems, or social-cultural challenges of English language learners to inform your diagnosis. Any of these approaches will inform your thinking about the case student and many others who may have similar characteristics.

Curriculum Case Study

In this type of case study, the instructional unit is the case. As with student case study, choose a unit of curriculum as the focus of your collaboration time and gather documentation to support the development, implementation, and evaluation of the curriculum unit. Some examples of work include integration of state standards into formative assessments, design of materials for students to use, linking concepts from one discipline to another, or developing a project-based learning activity that allows students to practice critical thinking skills. Curriculum work is often done by vertical and horizontal teams. Vertical teams might create a systematic sequence of instruction, activities, and assessments, whereas horizontal teams might strive for consistency between classrooms or share approaches to teaching similar content.

Following is an outline that can be used or modified by an individual or team for planning, implementation, or evaluation of curriculum.

Name: _____

Grade Level or Content Area: _____

Curriculum, School, or Staff

Reading instruction at XYZ Elementary School with other third-grade teachers

Teaching the concept of persuasive writing in a high school English class

Scope, Sequence, or Length

A six-week reading instruction unit

A four-week unit in ninth-grade English or language arts

Students Served

Whole class, with special emphasis on students who read well but don't write well

Heterogeneously grouped ninth graders

Assessments

Use standardized assessment data, textbook-based unit tests or writing assessments to determine where students need further instruction and plan second unit to follow your current unit. Use other available assessments from previous years for additional data sources.

Six-traits writing assessment or other writing assessment created by teachers

Standards

State reading standards

State ninth-grade writing standards or National Writing Project recommendations

Program Design

State-adopted reading instruction program is a standardized approach to teaching English and is widely used in large, urban districts. It is considered "direct instruction" and "scripted," and teachers are expected to work through the curriculum in very structured ways, with little room for variation.

Ninth-grade writing curriculum is designed to be taught alongside a novels curriculum. Students write one paper per three genres over three trimesters.

Assumptions About How Student Achievement Will Be Raised

The achievement data produced by reading unit assessments is thorough and explicit on some levels, ranking students against standards and against each other. The data are intended to be used for diagnostic purposes, so that instruction can be modified and differentiated as needed.

Teacher teams that include at least three grade levels review class sets of essays, identify anchor papers, and evaluate all ninth-grade papers. The rubric is taken from XYZ writing assessment materials, and students will be evaluated as advanced, proficient, at grade level, or below grade level. Students not meeting the standard will given additional writing instruction and will be asked to revise and resubmit their work.

Challenge

It is difficult to balance whole-group instruction with small-group instruction or "workshops," even though the curriculum is designed to be differentiated. The variation in student skill levels is great, ranging from newcomers with little English to English-only students performing at grade level or above. The gap between the lowest- and highest-performing students often widens through the year.

Goal

To modify the way I group students so that the lowest-performing students get more support earlier in the year. Two approaches I plan to try are for reading experiences:

1. Have parent volunteers read with students in their first language, and reading buddies will read with third graders and fifth graders.

2. Focus on vocabulary development using "realia" or pictures and artifacts to give students hands-on experience with the ideas in the unit.

Resources

Allen, D., *Assessing Student Learning: From Grading to Understanding* (New York: Teachers College Press, 1998).

This text is a collection of teachers' and facilitators' experiences using progressive student assessment approaches. The first-person reports on the challenges of establishing collaborative norms for honest evaluation of teaching and learning are instructive and cautionary.

Blythe, T., Allen, D., and Powell, B., *Looking at Student Work Together: A Companion Guide to Assessing Student Learning* (New York: Teachers College Press, 1999).

This guide is a good companion to the Allen text above, describing useful protocols and how to facilitate them in detail. The authors give examples of facilitation strategies, discuss processes for developing collaboration, and address the connection between teacher expertise and school change. The text contains additional resources.

Farr, S., *Teaching as Leadership: The Highly Effective Teacher's Guide to Closing the Achievement Gap* (San Francisco: Jossey-Bass, 2010).

This text builds a strong case for the power of individual teachers to lead change from the classroom out. Teach for America corps members report on the hard work of making classrooms places where learning happens. The craft of teaching is synthesized into key strategies that effective teachers use while still recognizing the importance of teacher partnerships beyond the classroom.

Hayes Jacobs, H., and Johnson, A., *The Curriculum Mapping Planner: Templates, Tools and Resources for Effective Professional Development* (Alexandria, Va.: ASCD, 2009).

This author and her colleague continue to update guidelines and tools for curriculum mapping. The mapping process is an invaluable process tool, providing artifacts and evidence for teachers conducting classroom-, school- or districtwide curriculum alignment. The focus on assessment continues to be useful in the context of standardized testing.

Schmuck, R., *Practical Action Research for Change*, 2nd ed. (Thousand Oaks, Calif.: Corwin Press, 2006).

Action research is a tried-and-true form of collaborative study in the context of the work. This author describes steps toward a collaborative inquiry process and offers examples of teacher teams and their inquiry efforts. This tradition is particularly helpful for those working across roles, such as teachers and parents or other community members.

Yin, R., *Case Study Research: Design and Methods*, 4th ed. (Thousand Oaks, Calif.: Sage, 2008).

The case study approach to school-based inquiry is helpful in defining the scope of an inquiry project, questions, participants, and settings. Now in its fourth edition, this text has proven itself as a theoretically sound source of information for a range of researchers. Cases can range from one student to a group of focus students to a department, leadership team, or school staff. Cases can also be framed around curriculum and assessment.

Notes

The epigraph to this chapter is drawn from J. Dewey, *Democracy and Education* (New York: McMillan, 1916).

1. A. G. Stone, R. F. Russell, and K. Patterson, "Transformational Versus Servant Leadership: A Difference in Leader Focus," *Leadership and Organization Development Journal* 25(4) (2004): 349–361 (quotation from p. 349).

2. F. Crowther, M. Ferguson, and L. Hann, *Developing Teacher Leaders: How Teacher Leadership Enhances School Success* (Thousand Oaks, Calif.: Corwin Press, 2007).

3. National Center for Education Statistics, *The Condition of Education: Contexts of Elementary and Secondary Education* (Washington, D.C.: National Center for Education Statistics, 2009).

4. M. Mangin and S. Stoelinga, *Effective Teacher Leadership: Using Research to Inform and Reform* (New York: Teachers College Press, 2007).

5. A. Howley, A. Solange, and J. Perry, "The Pain Outweighs the Gain: Why Teachers Don't Want to Become Principals," *Teachers College Record* 107(4) (2005): 757–782; L. Zinn, "Supports and Barriers to Teacher Leadership: Reports of Teacher Leaders," paper presented at the annual meeting of the American Educational Research Association, Chicago, March 1997. http://lsc-net.terc.edu/do.cfm/paper/8120/show/use_set-careers/page-3.

6. K. Leithwood, D. Jantzi, and R. Steinbach, *Changing Leadership for Changing Times* (Buckingham, U.K.: Open University Press, 1999; quotation from p. 116).

7. S. Mendez-Morse, *Leadership Characteristics That Facilitate School Change* (Austin, Tex.: SEDL, 1992). www.sedl.org/change/leadership.

8. S. Farr, *Teaching as Leadership: The Highly Effective Teacher's Guide to Closing the Achievement Gap* (San Francisco: Jossey-Bass, 2010).

9. P. Hallinger, "Leading Educational Change: Reflections on the Practice of Instructional and Transformational Leadership," *Cambridge Journal of Education* 33(3) (2003): 329–351.

10. Mendez-Morse, *Leadership Characteristics*, 1992.

11. D. Britzman, *Practice Makes Practice: A Critical Study of Learning to Teach*, 2nd ed. (New York: SUNY, 2003); M. Collay, "Recherche: Teaching Our Life Histories," *Teaching and Teacher Education* 14(3) (1998): 245–255; D. Lortie, *Schoolteacher* (Chicago: University of Chicago Press, 1975).

4

COLLABORATION IS LEADING

When those who have been excluded to the periphery get to
meet with those inside the system, it is always a wonderful
surprise to everyone to see how much they share in common
and how many of them want the same thing.

—*Margaret Wheatley*

The language that teachers use to characterize themselves
and others in relation to collaboration is powerful, persistent, and
worthy of further examination. The concept of *teaching as leading*
is based on the premise that designing and facilitating instruction in all its forms is a powerful form of educational leadership.
Collaborating with others is a natural extension of the quest to
create effective learning experiences for students. Having made
the commitment to teach students with integrity, one soon realizes the path is traveled in the company of others. The challenge for teachers is navigating informal and formal working
groups so that greater amounts of time and energy are spent with
those best positioned to do the most important work. Leading
for learning is a goal teachers share in common, and working in small teams creates conditions to obtain those goals. In
this chapter, my colleagues and I describe working groups that
support classroom instruction, recognize the need to balance
informal and formal collaborative structures, and make recommendations for ways to evaluate what's working and how to
establish or sustain effective collaboration.

Assumptions About Collaboration

Collaboration is a commonly used term, but systematic, productive collaboration is not common at all. Teachers are initially socialized to work solo in self-contained settings, one egg inside an egg carton. Most school schedules allow only an hour a week for formal team time, if that. Many teachers work well beyond the requirements of the contract, and much of that time is used for individual classroom preparation. Real collaboration time is rare. Well-structured collaboration is even scarcer. There is an adage among professional development coaches that "common prep time is required, but not sufficient" for teachers to learn together. Professionals need purposeful, focused time to talk about how to teach well, what to teach, and what the students know and don't know. The students they serve need teachers to collaborate on their behalf so the instruction provided aligns with their learning. Once carved out of the calendar, collaborative time must be structured in a systematic way, much as a good lesson plan or unit of instruction is organized. Collaboration time benefits from its own curriculum and deserves regular evaluation to ensure teachers are getting what they need. Creating and sustaining structures for collaboration are powerful and necessary forms of leadership. A quality design for professional development is essential.

Lambert's first assumption about leadership (see Chapter One) supports collaboration as leading. She writes: "Leadership may be understood as reciprocal, purposeful learning in community."[1] Professional collaboration for teaching and learning occurs primarily in response to improving classroom instruction and occurs at several levels: role-alike partners and teams, site-based working groups, and district-level reform efforts. In Chapter Three, my colleagues and I considered classroom-centered teaching and learning for both students and teachers. Student learning (or the lack of learning) in the classroom prompts teachers to engage colleagues in larger, more systemic responses. In this chapter, we consider formal site-based collaboration processes and structures that reframe the classroom as part of a larger system.

Establishing and sustaining structured collaboration time is a delicate dance among all the professionals at the site. In most cases, school leaders must make common planning time a priority or it doesn't happen. Once the time is created, it must then be protected for the real work of learning about teaching, not used for announcements, paperwork, or other bureaucratic tasks. Teacher-initiated planning is generally more productive than principal- or central office–dictated team time. Professionals themselves, not individuals outside the team, determine the focus of their collaboration and create or sustain working teams. The principal's role is essential: the calendar and instructional time must allow shared planning time. Framing schoolwide goals and mediating external pressures is also the role of the principal. How collaborative time is used and what work gets done is the province of teachers.

The term *professional learning community* has emerged over the last fifteen years, reflecting our desire to do all three: be professional, continue to learn, and to do our work in community with others. Hord reviewed literature examining school reforms enacted from the mid-1980s through the 1990s, with a particular focus on how successful educators transformed schooling.[2] Other researchers and staff developers have written about how to structure learning for adults working in schools and the necessary conditions for them to do so. Some of this work assumes that teachers are workers and must be "motivated" to work well together, while others take the perspective that professionals create and sustain our own learning.[3]

Learning circles, as we call them, "are small communities of learners among teachers and others who come together intentionally for the purpose of supporting each other in the process of learning."[4] Our thinking about learning circles was based on professional experiences of four educators from different educational traditions who had benefited from small, focused collaborations in a variety of settings. Learning circles are generally small working groups within larger communities of practice where learning about teaching is the focus.

I admire the work of Jean Lave and Etienne Wenger, who study "communities of practice."[5] Wenger defines communities of practice as "groups of people who share a concern or a passion for something they do and learn how to do it better as they interact regularly." He notes that "practice is the source of coherence" in this community, making it different from a neighborhood or a group of people gathered for nonwork reasons. Development of a community of practice leads to mutual engagement, a joint enterprise, and a shared repertoire.[6] The size, purpose, and scope of work undertaken by communities of practice in schools vary. Understanding the purpose and structure of working groups that make up the larger community is an essential element of leadership.

Collaborative Structures

In every school there exists what I call "naturally occurring" work teams. Rather than imposing a predetermined calendar or subcommittee structure, consider who already works together and for what purpose. Generally, we choose those who can help us get our work done. This may seem obvious, but I have observed that the majority of "meeting time" in most organizations is not structured for real or applied work. As in any organization, there are positive and negative sides of "relational teams." Naturally occurring pairs or small groups are usually driven by the task at hand and may also reflect friendships, patterns of hiring or work history, and cultural alliances. The point is to recognize patterns of affiliation and work consciously with, within, and around them.

Three commonly occurring work groups are pairs or partners, role-alike teams, and vertical or horizontal task-focused groups.

Role-alike teams might be the fourth-grade team or the English department. A vertical team might be the kindergarten though third-grade teachers working to align a curriculum sequence. A horizontal team might be five high school teachers from different disciplines who share a cohort of students. Whole staffs meet frequently or periodically in most schools, but very little real work is done in those settings. The reason large groups are not effective learning settings is not recalcitrance or mean-spiritedness—it is a problem of purpose and scope. If the purpose of the large-group session is focused and useful, participants will engage the essential ideas and then move into settings where the ideas can be applied. Think about the family dinner table compared to a family reunion. Some interesting conversations might occur at the reunion, but the real action happens in the kitchen after everyone else has left.

Partners or Pairs

My training as a teacher involved the use of cooperative learning in the classroom. My education about organizational development involved the facilitation of group processes from the ideal quintet through large staffs. I recall attending a workshop on "group work," where I learned about "knee to knee and eye to eye,"[7] the important first step in building trust with another. I still use pairs or dyads as the starting point for classes, school staffs, and colleagues at the university. Nothing is more powerful than sharing an idea, an experience, or an emotion with another human being. A three- to five-minute pair share can do wonders to reduce stress and build trust among staff members. A commonly shared curriculum concern that crosses all roles and personalities provides a useful prompt. A skillful prompt for pairs goes a long way in establishing positive community at a school.

With or without formal collaboration time, partners with shared interests find each other. Role-alike peer mentorship is the most common form of collaboration. It occurs informally and formally, with neighbors close by or with interest-alike colleagues at the site. Informal peer mentoring happens every day, every time one colleague shares an idea or asks for advice. More noticeable forms of mentoring occur when an experienced person offers professional support to a newcomer. Such support can occur in a specific instructional area, over the period of an instructional unit or through an entire school year. In educational settings, a more experienced person may offer mentoring one-on-one or within a team.

Talika describes her mid-career re-entry into work as a speech therapist and the teaching partner who supported her transition. "When I think back now, how did she perform her own job and answer all my questions, show me where everything was located, and even show me how to operate the copy machine?" Talika listed the many ways her mentor supported her development as a specialist, emphasizing her growing confidence and independence in the role. She closed with this telling point: "Thinking back, I do not remember the principal at that time. I imagine the principal was there at meetings and in the office, but I do not recall a principal offering suggestions or support. Our school has been through many administrative changes over the years, and most have had too many responsibilities other than being a principal. If it had not been for my peer mentor, I would have had a much more difficult time becoming reacquainted with the field."

Xavier described his painful first years teaching physical science in high school, including months of struggling with discipline and classroom management problems. He recalled almost losing his job after a poor evaluation: "Then something happened that I didn't think was possible. My department chair spoke up for me and made the VP remove that letter from the file. She and my evaluator said that I was working hard at teaching these tough classes and that I was doing what they recommended, so I should not to be punished for it."

His relationship with his chair was truly a make-or-break relationship for his professional induction. "From that point on,

I knew I was in teaching heaven, because others saw the value I had to offer. I have made a point of supporting new teachers so they didn't have to go through the rough years. I have to say that supportive science teachers here at my school made it possible for me to continue teaching."

The next example comes from Fiona, an experienced teacher with a new assignment who had asked a colleague to coach her on instruction. "One of my science colleagues works with teachers in the process of earning their National Board certification. She spends a great deal of her time outside of work helping teachers analyze their teaching practices for the betterment of their students. As such, she has been a great help to me as I adjust to teaching a single subject." I note that Fiona characterizes her colleague's coaching of other teachers as "time outside of work." Her words reflect the assumption that "work" is what teachers do with students, not what they do for colleagues. Fiona describes her colleague as knowledgeable about content and approaches to the craft of teaching and learning: "One of the things I really appreciate about her style is that all of her guiding questions are related to the students. She asked me about what they learned, how I knew what they learned, who didn't learn what I expected, and so forth. She really addressed the shift that I am currently in the process of making, from thinking about my teaching to thinking about their learning. Even though this really makes sense when you say it out loud, it's a difficult thing to do."

Partnering is the easiest and most naturally occurring collaboration, with good reason. The purpose is generally clear, and the outcome for students is evident. Collaboration in schools often begins with pairs building relationships in the direct service of classroom instruction. Teaching with a strong partner is a joy and improves learning experiences for the partners and their students.

There is a dark side to closely knit partners that must be addressed as teachers take responsibility to facilitate communities of practice. Partners are generally part of larger teams, and tightly bonded partners can float or sink their larger team. It's easy to spend planning time with a friend, not so easy with colleagues whose company we don't enjoy or who don't share our culture, history, or worldview. I consulted in an elementary school where the kindergarten team of three teachers had churned through a good handful of fourth members year after year. I pointed out this pattern to the principal and suggested she reconfigure the team membership before putting yet another newcomer into what had become an exclusive club of three.

Role-Alike Teams

Role-alike collaboration can be as easy as a friendship or as difficult as an arranged marriage. Collaboration is more comfortable when colleagues have a personal relationship, a shared work history, or other common life experiences. It is easier to establish team norms between individuals who need each other to complete a task or a large piece of work. Collaboration is more compelling when partners see a direct benefit to sharing parts of a larger whole, especially when that partnership produces real outcomes, will be viewed as successful, and becomes a foundation for other work, whatever the personality of the group. Here is a reflection from Shawna, a sixth-grade teacher reporting on her grade-level team's development of extracurricular activities: "We are a conscientious unit that enhances the lives of our students. As a group, we have implemented many programs that allow our students to grow, such as the basketball team, talent show, fiesta program, student council, science camp, lunchtime clubs, and enrichment program. Our students have benefited from the implementation of these programs."

This particular team works well together, and this teacher portrays her colleagues positively. "The best part of working with such a wonderful collaborative team is that everyone is dedicated and willing to help one another." When team members see each other through this lens, work gets accomplished and life is good. There is some danger of groupthink and exclusion of other, less like-minded colleagues, similar to the trio described earlier.

Experienced teachers invite, welcome, and depend on role-alike colleagues to craft curriculum, review assessments, and plan instruction. After identifying gaps and needs, many work across roles to improve educational processes throughout the school. Renee, another middle school teacher, describes the characteristics of her team, their expertise, and the nature of their leadership: "I collaborated with three other eighth-grade teachers. We are two females and two males, have multiple subject credentials, and are teaching two core classes of language arts and reading. After disaggregating our school data, we agreed to look at our below basic students and figure out how we could raise their scores. I chose this group to work with because they are all young teachers who are willing to look at data to help improve their teaching."

This team is on the same wavelength about using data to inform instruction, which is not always the case. I know from advising this team that they are not close friends outside of work, but they meet after school on a regular basis to ensure their instruction matches student needs. Exchanging ideas with those from whom we differ, either personally or professionally, is necessary for our students, our own learning, and for the development of the organization. Learning to work effectively with individuals who look different, have different cultural or language backgrounds, or who don't share the same worldview as ours is challenging and requires a professional integrity and belief in the task at hand. This commitment to working well with others is necessary as soon as we join a grade-level team or department.

In the next recollection, Renee offers a common scenario of collaboration. This team chose to meet, selected the focus of their inquiry, and were each invested in the outcome, yet they did not come to consensus without a struggle. "I have learned that it necessary for group members to disagree and be able to move forward toward a common goal. My inquiry group has dealt with many issues due to basic differences in personality, learning, and working styles. I can recall vividly occasions when my group has not been "on the same page" due to these differences. Many times our working sessions have turned into heated discussions between one person's view and another's."

Renee stayed the course, however, noting her shift toward more balance: "As a result of working through these situations, I have realized the importance of listening to the needs of others along with voicing my own." She describes her maturation as a leader as she both listens to others and expresses her own opinions. "Through talking out many of these difficult situations, it is possible for everyone's voice to be heard and validated without compromising their beliefs."

Taking the lead in collaborative settings shows the importance of support and validation among the individuals in the group. Temporary leaders also need cooperation from the group to take the lead in certain circumstances, for certain projects, or for certain periods of time. "Shared leadership" is much harder than working in a hierarchy, where one person is assigned the task of "managing" others. Productive teaching teamwork requires a high level of commitment from individuals to each other, to the process, and to the learners. Productive teams have different leaders for different tasks. As Patricia, a third-grade bilingual teacher, describes, "A leader is not a person who gives orders or works alone to complete a task. A leader is a person who works collaboratively with other teachers for the common good of the school." Such rotation of shared leadership is not easy. A middle school teacher reflects on her experience sharing leadership within a group: "Working in a group required a lot more work than what I initially believed. I have become very aware that, as people and leaders, we all require different support structures. I realize that through all our differences we still share the common desire for respect and the opportunity for our feelings to be validated. Working with my group has taught me an irreplaceable lesson about the way I work with others in and outside of a school setting."

Hundreds of books have been written about leading and following, many holding the assumption that to be a leader, one must have followers. Like many others, I question the conventional wisdom that it takes a charismatic leader with eager followers to transform a school. On the other hand, for shared leadership to be healthy in the best case and possible in the worst case, each of us must be willing to publicly acknowledge and appreciate our colleagues who offer their expertise. True role-alike leadership doesn't occur when individuals sit together but do not share membership. It's easy enough to be critical of a person or an idea. Leading means supporting others through the process of building trust and making room for consensus to occur. Following does not have to mean going along with ideas or processes that fall outside our values.

Task-Focused Teams

Productive collaboration grows out of need and purpose. Having a valid task and a clear purpose for coming together is essential and makes a group a team. Task-focused work is powerful compared to groups meeting out of habit or even because the group is likely to need collaborative time. I use the activities offered in a ropes course as an example of group process for its own sake. While it's helpful to work as a team to make sure each member gets across the rope bridge safely, such teamwork does not automatically transfer into the everyday work setting. Generally, people who need each other to get work done will find ways to collaborate. Completing real work together strengthens ties and helps build trust. Collaboration focused on specific projects or systems maintains a sense of purpose.

Andrea, an experienced kindergarten teacher who transferred to a neighboring school when her school closed, described a project that helped her establish membership in the new staff: "In partnership as leaders, we improved the quality of our teaching for our students while increasing on-site collegiality. As a new member of the school staff, I see the value and importance of building positive and constructive working relationships so that important decisions that affect our site are made with honesty and clear communication in order to come to a consensus."

Andrea talked about improved teaching as directly benefiting all students. She also noted positive outcomes for her colleagues. Focused collaboration leads to better learning for students and a stronger community of practice for teachers.

Productive teams often begin by analyzing their own students' data, then looking for schoolwide patterns that can inform their team's decision making. Here is a reflection from a teacher who looked at assessment data with her grade-level team. Fran described "presenting the data about poor performance of the school's English learners, and my grade-level team came up with a few suggestions. Teachers need to educate our parents about English language development, helping children with homework, and aiding children's positive behavior." This team also came up with the suggestion that "our district offer more preschools so that our English learners have a better chance at success."

Task-driven teams often require vertical or horizontal configurations that become formal or de facto leadership teams. These teams can be councils, in that they represent roles or role-alike members like department chairs at a high school. They can be vertical teams that include, for instance, a representative from every grade level in the school. The intent is that each constituent group is represented at the table where the decisions are made. These leadership teams are as effective as the purpose of the collaboration, the method used to determine membership, and the visibility of the outcome to those they purport to represent. Horizontal teams, for instance, lead theme-based curriculum at the secondary level that includes one teacher from each discipline.

Vertical teams in elementary schools are not common, but they are critical to the establishment of communities of practice. As students progress through the grades, they are passed along from one small container inside the egg carton to the next. It is essential to their success that their teachers work together effectively to align and strengthen the scope and sequence of the curriculum. In the next example, Tina describes her transition to the role of grade-level team representative: "At the beginning of this year, I was asked and agreed to be on a schoolwide leadership team which is currently conducting an inquiry on English language arts and writing." She describes her role as mediator between her grade level and the rest of the leadership team: "My team had different opinions about grading the writing. I heard the opinions of my second-grade team and expressed their concerns at my next meeting. I presented a solution to accommodate the second grade and the rest of the staff. The staff was happy with the outcome."

As a representative, Tina took her team's concerns to the schoolwide decision-making group, but she also "presented a solution," indicating her willingness to advocate for her team's approach in the larger collective. She returned to her team not only having represented them, but also having influenced the larger community with their expertise.

In this next excerpt, Anita, a middle school teacher, conducted an equity audit developed by the Association of California School Administrators. The association's Position Paper and Audit Tool (see Chapter Five) are useful in assessing the quality of professional relationships at a school. The assessment profile considers curriculum, recruitment, hiring and coaching practices, community engagement, support structures, resources, leadership, and relationships. "We held a meeting with all seventh and eighth teachers and discussed the audit tool. From our collaboration, we found this tool to be useful in facilitating a meeting. Our goals were to evaluate classroom practices and develop an action plan for the Full English Proficiency transition process. We plan to meet again after all data is collected and recommendations are prepared, then share our recommendations and guide teachers through this process."

There was some conversation with the principal and a consultant to set up the middle school professional development process, but the weekly meetings were led by teachers. Knowing the team's strengths and capacity to consider information within the data allowed this teacher to work effectively with her middle school colleagues. After gaining a foothold with the smaller team, two teachers moved outward to the school leadership team to enlist their support and to educate them about the need to upgrade the status of students who were previously assessed as English language learners and had since become proficient in English. "We collaborated with our site's English learner specialist, principal, vice principal, student services coordinator, and resource specialist. The increase in communication among us, in regard to English learner processes, was outstanding. We looked into the state guidelines and district guidelines much more, and we have filled gaps created by the system."

When individuals are able, they position themselves by interest, topic, and potential to succeed. They work with those who share interests or are willing to do certain work. As mentioned earlier, the teams can be formal or informal, but they are most effective when collaborating around a shared purpose. Laura described a formal "appointed" group that is productive and the experience reciprocal: "They just also happen to be my appointed language arts team as well. As language arts teachers, we are responsible for teaching all of our writing genres according to the standards, so it made sense to approach them with my ideas and facts. I found them receptive and more than willing to sit with me and use department time to look at the data. They cared, too. I walked away with additional insights about common assessments that we could use for progress assessments in writing and reading."

This team was effective in leading curriculum development because members were working with real information—standards, test scores, and observation. In earlier times, teachers had fewer tools and guidelines at hand and less experience working with discrete data. Teams can collaborate more effectively if the framework is transparent and the standards offer a baseline for what students should be able to do. A leadership team member offered this description of her work leading peer observations at her school:

> For example, my team members and I created a PowerPoint presentation to give our project participants a sense of purpose and meaning for their teaching. We therefore needed to have thoughtful discussions and make a thorough analysis of the data collected from their surveys in order to inform our participants with good information that would guide their participation in the process. The three of us felt so empowered by the end of our planning meeting, it was truly an example of high-level collaboration. Each of us was able to contribute great ideas. When we came to an obstacle, we solved problems with respect, flexibility, and focus.

This teacher captured the power of "high-level collaboration" when her team gathered data, talked about the data, and planned ways to bring colleagues into the process. "Respect, flexibility, and focus" capture thoughtful processes that sustain a community of practice. Andrea includes teacher collaboration and student outcomes in her characterization of leading through teaching: "I plan to continue working with others towards closing the achievement gap in our school. If I decide to seek employment in another school, my goal is to continue to advocate for students who are not being served as they should be. As a leader, I always take into consideration the needs of the staff, and most importantly the students, because they are the reason why I chose teaching as my profession."

Andrea's values are sound, yet are often lost in the daily grind of management. Like many of us, she chose teaching because of the students. Teachers who keep students at the center of their practice must engage in many forms of leadership and varying configurations of leadership teams. Over the last thirty years, educational reformers have increasingly borrowed from other fields to inform thinking about who can lead schools and to reconsider how teachers lead.[8] Variously called school-based management or distributed, collective, or shared leadership, among other terms, the nature of school leadership has evolved to a more collaborative, team-based approach.

Sharing Professional Responsibility for Learning

Sharing expertise is the most powerful form of leadership, whatever one's title. Some research suggests that teachers seeking to improve their own practice look to individuals with specific areas of expertise. Often that person is a peer with whom we have a relationship. Spillane, Hallett, and Diamond studied distributive leadership in urban schools and found that individual teachers identified "leadership" through the social construct of capital (cultural, social, human, and economic): "Our account illustrates how the construction of leadership is situated in different interactions, with teachers constructing different leaders according to the subject area; constructing school administrators as leaders largely on the basis of cultural capital; and constructing teachers as leaders of the basis of cultural, social, and human capital."[9]

This idea fits with Wenger's conception of communities of practice, particularly "mutual engagement." He believes that "practice exists because people are engaged in actions whose meanings they negotiate with one another."[10] Such research compels us to continually question our notions of expertise and professional development models that do not recognize teachers as leaders of learning.

Teachers work effectively in many group configurations, from team-teaching pairs to large departments. Many teachers, however, are quite conflicted about entering each other's classrooms for the purposes of supporting instructional practice. The transition from talking about students, curriculum, and assessment to spending time in a colleague's classroom is a large one. Research on communities of practice considers essential characteristics in the development of professionalism within a work group. These characteristics include: problem solving, requests for information, seeking experience, reusing assets, coordination and synergy, discussing developments, documentation projects, visits, and mapping knowledge and identifying gaps.[11] "Visits" jumped off the page when I reviewed this list. Productive collaborators in schools engage in most of the items identified, yet the missing one is often "visiting each other's classroom." Unless we team-teach on a regular basis, having a colleague observe or co-teach with us can be unsettling. I believe the more common cultural norm of adult isolation is partially responsible for this discomfort. I also believe that teaching others is an extremely personal and individualistic endeavor. While most of us have felt the sting of criticism from students or colleagues at one time or another over our careers, I don't think those experiences are the key reason we distance ourselves from the chance to engage in real dialogue about instructional practice. The staff-management metaphor limits healthy interaction between colleagues.

An important step toward blurring the boundaries of hierarchy is recognizing the structures that create them. Conventional practices of teacher evaluation, for example, are based on a supervisory model: the principal is the supervisor whose task is to "see over," and the teachers are being "seen over." This unfortunate management stance isn't suited to improving teaching practice and is only appropriate when documentation of unethical behavior is needed to remove a teacher from the classroom. Novice teachers are coached not to take risks during their early years' evaluations, but to present a very tight, foolproof lesson. Experienced teachers generally continue the pattern because both teacher and principal know the formal evaluation is a legal matter, not a process intended to support professional development. Even when there is trust between principal and teacher, both realize the formal evaluation is required by contract, and both parties generally do their part to make sure the documentation is in order and both sides are protected.[12]

"Peer observation" is a hybrid term that aptly captures the conflicted experience of teachers seeking peer review or peer support in the classroom. On the positive side, most teachers want a trusted colleague to give helpful feedback. On the negative side, "observation" presumes one teacher *watches* another, takes notes, and gives written feedback. While this level of feedback can be useful, the process of providing helpful feedback is only as useful as the relationship between the players and the quality of partnership in which the feedback occurs. Without trust, authentic risk taking will not happen.

There are helpful guidelines for initiating peer exchange, as I prefer to call the process of being in another teacher's space during instructional time. Both parties must agree it's a good idea, the purpose for the exchange must be clear, and there must be agreement on whether notes will be taken. Any notes should remain with the host teacher. The host teacher sets the time, place, and terms. The guest teacher does what is needed to reassure the host that it is a safe and trustworthy process. The guest must therefore keep all opinions to herself until there is a foundation of shared understanding upon which to build candid conversation. Developing such trust may take several months or even years. The terms "host and guest" are hardly professional terms, but the management framework of supervision and evaluation must be disrupted before truly collaborative observation exchanges can be put in place.

Early experiences with peer exchange should be short and sweet, with a very low-stakes focus. The host teacher can and should be very direct with her guest. For instance, I always invite a colleague I trust to "observe" or co-teach material that I know well. I use approaches or activities in which I am confident. After working with someone over a longer time, it is easier to take a walk on the wild side and try things that are risky. After developing a history of safe, even-handed peer exchanges, a foundation of trust will be in place to support authentic critique and suggestions about ways to improve practice.

Niko, a teacher who values regular peer feedback and goes out of his way to invite others into his fourth-grade room, describes the process and the value: "Peer observation is a powerful resource and tool to develop an educator's pedagogy for more effective teaching and instruction. Having less formal but structured opportunities to observe and evaluate each other is useful for the recognition and understanding of methods and practices that are working effectively. Being in a nonthreatening setting with familiar and trusted colleagues enables teachers to be more open and objective in our own assessments and analysis. This option encourages educators to be more aware and conscious of our own performance, helping us to self-examine and modify strategies and systems appropriately."

Niko captured the tension in the oxymoron "peer observation" by describing the need for it to be less formal and structured at the same time. Notions of peer observation are tainted by our experiences with contract-driven evaluation, especially if we were "watched" as we struggled with behavior problems or we lacked confidence or experience with course content. Few of us can say we have positive experiences with a supervisory review. "Inviting" a peer to exchange support and reflection, however, moves us away from watching over or being watched toward a trustworthy collaboration that strengthens the practice of both participants.

There can be some antipathy for a colleague who steps away from exclusive peer membership by way of a changed title, status, or role. Remember the historic tension for teachers about whether they are professionals or staff who report to management. This unfortunate stratification limits leadership development for everyone. First, some might be concerned they will be seen as "other" or seen as siding with management, should they choose or be asked to take on specialized roles. Second, those who naturally distrust supervisors will distance themselves from the decision or the appointed colleague. Third, predictable professional jealousy emerges in some cases, and the anointed one may be challenged by others who believe they have similar or greater skills. Socialization into more formal leadership can be subtle or blatant, but any formal recognition of "leader" status changes one's relationship to colleagues.

Collaborating Across Roles

Formal team leadership changes the culture of the group and the individual leader's role. A formal decision about leadership moves individuals from informal activity that may be invisible beyond the team to a more visible role with a title, such as grade-level leader or department chair. These leaders are sometimes appointed by an administrator, sometimes nominated by peers, and sometimes self-appointed. At the secondary level, department chairs in larger middle or high schools often are elected, have budget authority, and may have formal training or an administrative credential. Positional leadership, or taking a role with a name, changes how we see ourselves and how others see us. Some of the leadership literature addresses characterizations of positional leadership and distributed leadership: "Equating leadership with the actions of those in leadership positions is inadequate for three reasons. First, leadership practice typically involves multiple leaders, some with and some without formal leadership positions. It is essential, therefore, to move beyond viewing leadership in terms of superhuman actions. Second, leadership practice is not something done to followers. From a distributed perspective, followers are one of the three constituting elements of leadership practice. Third, it is not the actions of individuals, but the interactions among them, that are critical in leadership practice."[13]

Formal appointment by the positional leader or to positional leadership can be useful and problematic at the same time. For instance, if our colleague is asked to take the lead on an accreditation effort, the rest of us are relieved not to be doing that work and will generally support the person, if not the task. Our colleague can blame the institution and be forgiven. In another case, if our colleague is appointed to lead a reform effort that is unpopular or not supported by a few or most of the others, major conflicts may arise. The individual will be accused of representing the institution, rather than her colleagues. Others feel that their expertise has been devalued and the "leader" isn't collaborating on behalf of the learner. Movement into formal positions often begins with added responsibilities such as principal for the day, teacher on special assignment, or content-based coaching. That colleague who takes "elevated" tasks we associate with positional leaders or supervisors becomes the "other"—someone we associate with management. We must continually examine our assumptions about the inherent nature of roles, leading, following, and collaboration. Recognize that organizations may seem to have a life of their own, but they are us. Resist the tendency to judge the motivation of others striving to do work. We are all members of evolving organizations and can build productive learning communities together.

Successful teachers collaborate with positional leaders on behalf of students. If we truly keep students' needs at the center of our practice, we can't stay inside the four walls of our classrooms. We are members of a larger community of practice and benefit from cross-role collaboration in every instance. In the next case, Larry describes a curriculum project that was district-initiated and supported and a productive experience for the team. "After the collaborative effort to learn a new language arts curriculum, we felt closer as a team and in unison. We all worked collectively toward closing the achievement gap between language minority and English-only students. We appreciated the support of the administration during three days of missing our regular classroom duties to embark on this new task. Without the support of the principal and district office, I do not think that this time to work collaboratively would have occurred."

Teachers who are successful acknowledge the complex systems of which they are a part. This colleague appreciated the learning opportunity created by the central office leadership, rather than characterizing the experience as top-down. The interplay between site-based and district-based leadership must be reciprocal. While there are few obvious channels through which teachers can influence district-level policy, those who work directly with students know more about policy needs than anyone else. Influence between parts of the system should go both ways.

In the next excerpt, Lucinda recognizes the limitations of current instructional approaches for her students and others like them and has strengthened her position with research. She acknowledges the need to participate in the larger debate, not just apply her findings in her own classroom: "Being equitable within the four walls of my classroom will not suffice either. I also need to branch out and work toward equity on my campus and beyond. Presently there is much research supporting harsh English-only programs for English language learners. This research seems convincing, but it has been poorly conducted and is misleading. I have had to counter these claims with other, more thorough research."

Teachers don't always have the experience of being heard by building-level and centralized leadership. In Lucinda's case, her expertise was recognized by her principal, who then asked her for more information. "For example, last year my principal approached me with data on the 'success' of two-way programs that had reduced the amount of Spanish instruction. He was considering the benefits of revising our 90–10 model in favor of a 50–50 model. He wanted to discuss the idea with the staff. I had to pull out research that demonstrated that changing our model would only produce short-term gains in standardized testing. It would not benefit our students."

A strong bilingual curriculum and assessment background gave this teacher firm ground on which to take a stand in critiquing a proposed reform. Teachers often find themselves holding expertise about a subject area or a reform effort, and a colleague who is less knowledgeable will approach us to learn from that expertise. A wise colleague recognizes that expertise and makes good use of it. In the next example, Yvette describes her curriculum activism at the district level: "Presently I am working toward changing how our district accepts students into the dual immersion program. Recent Spanish-speaking immigrants are being placed into English-only classrooms and are denied the primary language resources we have on our campus. This is a difficult issue because many staff members feel that they are doing what is best for the students, and influential English-speaking parents want those dual immersion spots for their children. I am gathering support from colleagues, bringing up discussion with administrators, and plan to continue to work at resolving this inequity."

In another example, a team of teachers is working at the district level to share expertise in language acquisition of primary grade students. Through district-level training, Tom, a member of the team, is learning leadership strategies that are useful at the site and beyond: "As a present representative of the Instructional Leadership Academy for our site, we practice leadership in a large setting with the superintendent, district administrators, and other teacher leaders. I have engaged in various discussions alongside these individuals and informed decisions that affect our students. The skills and knowledge that I have developed in community building and collaboration have transferred into my daily interactions and conversations with peers. I check my own background knowledge before I make a point to see if

I have researched the topic and can be more informative in my conversations."

As in previous examples, content expertise provides this leader credibility that extends beyond her school and into the larger system. Teachers often decry policy decisions that emanate from the central office and are research-light and politics-heavy. Decisions aren't always based on background knowledge, especially the kinds of knowledge that comes from focused, formal study.

Collaborating with Families

Teachers see children every weekday for many months of the year. In the case of younger children, teachers may see family members as part of the package. Building relationships with parents is a natural part of teaching young children, but becomes less common as children grow. As a middle school teacher, I only saw the parents of students who had serious discipline problems, and those parents weren't especially happy to make my acquaintance. As a parent of two middle school students, I am experiencing firsthand the other side of "co-parenting" or working collectively with my children's teachers. As a former secondary teacher, I know the impossibility of building relationships with 150 students and their families. Even the most experienced teachers can be overwhelmed by the workload and the number of students they see every day. I try to reserve my parent input for concerns that are worthy of follow-up. Although my children's teachers make me welcome, I remain cautious about how much contact is appropriate. My anxiety about disrupting the norms of mainstream schooling discourages me from seeking relationships with teachers. Our system doesn't readily support teachers and parents working together.

In spite of an organizational culture that limits parent-teacher collaboration, many of my colleagues succeed in creating partnerships with parents. Most of the stories come from elementary school settings, reflecting the patterns of greater parent involvement when students are young. Following are some examples of their leadership. We can learn from their successes and think creatively about how to initiate and maintain partnership with our children's teachers. Parents are indeed children's first and primary teachers, and teachers and parents can agree on the importance of educating each child.

Teachers in urban settings are often in the position of educating the parents about how schools work and how parents can navigate schooling. Advocating for parents who may not have cultural capital in the school setting can be a large part of the work of teaching in such settings. In the next excerpt, the teacher is on special assignment working directly with parents through a parent education class. While most classroom teachers have little opportunity to work with groups of parents, Lisa's experience is instructive, especially as it relates to the porous and conflicted boundary between parenting and teaching: "My students are parents of preschoolers in the state preschool program who are required to participate in their child's class once a week and attend a parent education class once a month. I teach these classes on a variety of topics such as positive communication, domestic violence, positive discipline, and how to help your child learn at home. I serve a total of six sites throughout the district, with classes ranging from twenty to fifty students."

Lisa is an experienced classroom teacher and the parent of two young children. She ruefully notes the hypocrisy in judging other parents for behaviors in which she herself engages: "My administrator advised me on how to teach these classes, reminding me of the importance of telling the parents not to let their children watch television. My reality is that television at times helps keep me sane as a parent as well as shows my child things that I cannot show him in person."

As a middle-class white woman, she will not be judged as an inadequate parent because her children are watching *Dora the Explorer* while she fixes dinner. Her colleague felt free to judge parents who had been identified as needing state services because of their poverty. In this case, parents are fulfilling the requirement to attend parenting classes: "My colleague who previously taught these classes talks about 'the poor parents' that didn't know to leave the materials in the classroom and who would appreciate donations from us, the parents with more material wealth. Some of the parents I teach are in serious economic situations and yet I have learned from and alongside them."

Lisa articulated the power of sharing the parenting struggle across class and race and the need to acknowledge common dilemmas and cooperate to improve her own and others' parenting skills: "By sharing our ideas together, we create new knowledge and understandings for all. I believe that we are the best parents for our children, and we can always try to learn to be more creative, more patient, and more self-assured in our parenting skills."

Initially, Lisa found the work of teaching parents directly very difficult. Roaming around the district without organizational support was challenging, and she felt ineffective. After making connections to district-level offices and some leaders who understood her goals, she now feels positioned to effect change beyond one school and one staff to a community and to parents. "Working as a parent educator without colleagues that shared my same job description, I found it difficult to enact the larger changes needed to address school and institutional change. I feel like I now have been charged with leading for change and my input is valued by my principal and colleagues."

The notion of parents as partners is foreign to some teachers, just as the possibility of truly teaming with their child's teacher may be a reach for some parents. Parents teach and teachers parent, yet we remain worlds apart when we have every reason to sit together on behalf of our children. Because I teach at night, I have the privilege of walking my child to school when many other parents are already at work. Some of my most powerful learning experiences about schooling have occurred over the past several years when I talk to my children's teachers on the yard before school. Those brief check-ins are priceless. Together we are bookends, holding my children together.

Advocating for parents who lack cultural capital in the school setting can be dangerous to a teacher's standing with colleagues. Tensions between parents and teachers are common, as educators strive to do their job in poorly funded schools. In this situation, Annamarie, an early years' teacher but a mature activist, used her expertise to confront others' beliefs about educating Spanish-speaking students. "I was marginalized by most teachers at my site. The opposition to a bilingual model was huge. I worked hard, I built bridges with Spanish-speaking families, bridges that I am proud to say are still strong twelve years later. During my second year, an outstanding teacher was hired to continue to build the bilingual program. We were two inexperienced teachers against the world, but we prevailed!"

Annamarie carries strong cross-cultural and bilingual credentials, which is the foundation of her role as a mediator of education for non-English speakers. Her vision is clear, and she is courageous in her stance. In the next excerpt, Mary describes a similar effort to advocate for parents. Mary is a product of the poor, working-class community where she teaches and does not feel socially well positioned to challenge the status quo, but she does so anyway: "I always found it very easy to speak to my students about equity and the rights that they have as students, while finding it more challenging to discuss the same rights with their parents. Feeling that parents need to know their rights, I reflected deeply on how to inform them in an ethical way. I read a lot of research about what my legal rights and responsibilities were, and soul-searched about how to arm my parents with the ammunition they needed to defend their children's rights."

Mary's use of a military metaphor as she describes "arming parents with ammunition" tells the tale of parents in this setting. I see images of combatants fighting against a large army. Her choice of words reflects her belief that parents find schools to be a war zone. She continues: "I educated my parents about the rights for a good education in an environment that is safe and secure for our children and told them where to go to be heard on the inequities in our district. I encouraged parents to defend their rights. While some other teachers were angered by this process, I have no regrets. Our parents need to learn to speak up when they feel that their children are not receiving the education they expect and deserve."

Mary's depiction of other educators' anger about her encouragement of parent activism raises questions about the purpose of schooling and ways of leading. Leaders in most settings are praised for challenging the status quo, yet teachers who advocate for underserved families may themselves be marginalized. Their stance may place them at odds with positional leaders for creating a political headache and with peers for adding additional pressures to an already pressure-filled role.

In the next vignette, a teacher team is working on a parent outreach program intended to raise student achievement. Carol describes "planning lessons with my partner teachers to expand and deepen a range of teaching strategies that engage every student in working hard at important things and to work towards closing the achievement gap." Her team developed a "series of assessments for our grade level to identify which students are succeeding and to provide focused intervention for those that are not." The focused intervention includes parent engagement: "We are designing a parent workshop to encourage working together for student success. This workshop will continue to build partnerships with parents through active outreach, inclusion, and two-way communication. By developing an understanding of the roles of parents, teachers, and students, together we will ensure that perspectives and experiences of underserved students appropriately influence changes in teaching and school practices."

Here is a teacher-led effort to include parents to improve student learning. I note with interest her use of "two-way communication" with parents. The phrase itself implies that previous communication was one-way or perhaps absent. The fact that this team needs to be so purposeful about changing norms of parent communication is illuminating.

Teachers and parents may need to overcome cultural, language, and class barriers to work effectively together. In most elementary schools, teachers are white women, working- or middle-class, and more educated than the families they serve. In many middle-class communities, teachers are less affluent than the families they serve and drive into the school from outlying areas because they can't afford to live where they teach. Some teachers do not characterize their work as "service," but as a job. Some are critical of families who may not be positioned to parent in middle-class ways or to come to school on the teacher's schedule. Parents may have histories of disenfranchisement from school and may not wish to relive the indignities they suffered as children and young people. Teachers who can reach through these barriers are leaders for equity and weave a stronger web of support for their students and families. They do so every day.

Collaboration is easier said than done, but it's much more doable when organized and led by teachers. Recognize the informal, useful exchanges with colleagues as vital to the work. Appreciate colleagues who are supporters, mentors, and guides. Extend the concept of collaboration beyond the school site to other settings. Communities of practice exist everywhere and can be nurtured and grown with attention. Start where you are and create what you and your students need.

Considerations About Collaboration as Leading

- Pay attention to when and how you meet with colleagues, including role-alike peers, specialists, and positional leaders. Spend more time doing what is most useful.
- Treat colleague meeting time as equal in value to instructional minutes.

- Evaluate how meeting time is planned, organized, and evaluated, and by whom.
- Set the agenda with those most invested in productive outcomes. Resist add-on bureaucratic activity, and advocate for student-centered work.
- Use student work to focus the agenda (see Chapters Three and Five for examples of teacher-led inquiry). Limit time spent on larger-scale projects that focus on textbooks, general standards, or large data sets.
- Share your learning, findings, protocols, and successes with colleagues, administrators, families, and the community.
- Strive to see parents as partners.

✑ INQUIRY FOUR ✑
Collaborations Small and Large

Collaboration is essential to learning anything, and learning to teach well is a lifelong endeavor. Start where you are by recognizing the places and spaces you already collaborate in your daily life. Small informal teams are often the most successful because they arise from need, focus on a specific problem to be solved, and depend on relationships. They can also be exclusive and have a limited impact on the larger organization. Larger, more formal collaborations can be successful, but need more structure and attention to process. I believe both small and large collaborations are necessary for individuals and the organization to grow. Use graphic organizers to provoke discussion and nurture the seeds of your learning community.

Professional Development Mapping and Analysis

Start where you are. I like to use a type of graphic organizer I call a circle-gram as an analytical tool (see Figure 4.1). It helps the author or team identify existing or potential collaboratives. It can be used to document and evaluate the relationships within your community of practice. It can also be used to analyze the relationships of projects to each other. The circle-gram is also useful to identify informal work groups at your site. Often teams develop around shared interests that don't follow predictable vertical or horizontal patterns. Modify the one in Figure 4.1 as needed or use a Venn diagram with overlapping areas if that approach is more useful.

Circle-Gram of Professional Support   Here are more examples of ways to use the circle-gram for levels of analysis:

1. Put your own name in the center, and identify up to six individuals (with real names and roles) to whom you look for support. The purpose of this activity is to recognize and

Figure 4.1 Circle-Gram

Circle-gram Author(s):

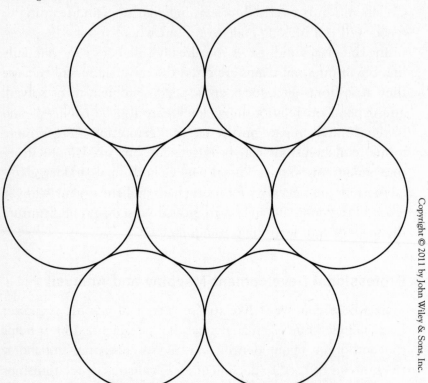

Purpose of the activity:

Uses for the information:

embrace those who actually serve as thinking partners, helpers, advisors, and teachers. These individuals might be members of your closest team, those who teach students before or after you, administrators who support your work, and friends or family members who also offer you professional support.

2. Put the name of your work group in the center and place yourself and your group members around the outside circle. In most cases, these will be the members of your grade-level team or your department. In some cases, the groups are heterogeneous, such as a vertical team of kindergarten though second-grade teachers who work with bilingual students or a multidisciplinary high school team that works with a cluster of students.

3. Put a topic of inquiry in the center and identify individuals, roles, or departments to contact in creating or strengthening your collaboration. Often the expertise exists on the staff, but the pathway to that expertise is not immediately obvious.

4. Put your department members inside the circles and ask each of them to list three collaborators from around the school. This graphic displays the existing connections that can be drawn upon for support. With some analysis, missing links or gaps become apparent and the team can decide which steps to take to close the gap. For instance, if the social studies team works regularly with the English department, but not the science department, to integrate curriculum, then social studies and English can set up more regular meetings and one or both can invite the science chair to join the team and bring in a third group of teachers. If everyone names the instructional technology teacher as a resource, but that individual is never invited to meetings, such an omission can be addressed.

5. Put a curriculum goal in the center and identify individuals or groups who have expertise relevant to the goal. For example, strengthening writing at the secondary level is always an area of concern, and different disciplines approach the problem in different ways. Put "writing curriculum" in the middle and invite different departments to fill in the circles. In a meeting of chairs, each might describe writing activities from their department and look for connections, instructional approaches, or teacher expertise to support improvement in all departments.

Use the circle-gram or other graphic organizers to document your personal and professional networks, schoolwide initiatives, or leadership team activity.

Curriculum Map and Calendar   Referring to the work of Heidi Hayes Jacobs[14] or your school or district guidelines, create a graphic organizer to document existing professional development opportunities, patterns, and configurations at the site.

1. Choose a map that allows you to document daily, weekly, monthly, and term professional development events. I recommend four- or six-week units, depending on how instruction is organized at the school or within the department.

2. Write in formal meetings that occur each day, week, month, and term.

3. Conduct an analysis. Who meets? What is the purpose of the meeting? Who sets up, facilitates, documents, and follows up? How does the work done at the meeting influence classroom practice?

4. Revise the map for the next unit or term. Modify the pattern to align meeting activity with teachers' goals and schoolwide, agreed-upon work.

Resources

Center on School, Family, and Community Partnerships.
www.csos.jhu.edu/p2000/center.htm

Joyce Epstein is known for her research and writing about schools, families, and community. This extensive web site has links to parent education information, articles, abstracts, and resources. It also offers links to conferences and workshops for teachers and parents or others seeking to build partnerships.

Collay, M., Dunlap, D., Enloe, W., and Gagnon, G., *Learning Circles: Creating Conditions for Teacher Professional Development*. Thousand Oaks, Calif.: Corwin Press, 1998.

This text draws from organizational development, adult learning theory, and communities of learning literature. The coauthors present their experiences participating in and leading small-group processes to support professional development. The chapters are developmental, showing the relationship and interactions between smaller subgroups, larger units, and whole staffs.

National Staff Development Council (now Learningforward).
www.learningforward.org/index.cfm

This web site is resource-rich and practitioner-friendly. In addition to providing links to conferences, workshops, and other sources of expertise, the site contains many accessible publications about current events, professional development frameworks, curriculum and instruction, assessment, and partnerships. The site provides a good centerpiece for professional development activities at a school or district.

National Equity Project (formerly BayCES).
www.bayces.org/article.php/Coachtools

The National Equity Project is a nonprofit organization based in Oakland, California, and its mission is leadership development, with a particular emphasis on creating equitable conditions in urban schools. The senior leadership team and school-based coaches have decades of experience as classroom teachers, coaches, policy developers, and partners in a range of districts throughout the country. Coaching resources are also available.

Teacher Leaders Network.

www.teacherleaders.org

This web site was created by a national network focused on developing the profession of teaching. Links connect to various levels of educational reforms, survey data—such as the Metropolitan Life Survey of Teachers—and international studies that can inform American educators—such as research on the Programme for International Student Assessment. The site includes interpretations of current reform efforts and studies through blogs and opinion pieces.

Notes

The epigraph to this chapter is drawn from M. Wheatley, "Bringing Schools Back to Life: Schools as Living Systems," *Creating Successful School Systems: Voices from the University, the Field, and the Community* (Norwood, Mass.: Christopher-Gordon, 1999).

1. L. Lambert, "Leadership Redefined: An Evocative Context for Teacher Leadership," *School Leadership and Management* 23(4) (2003): 421–430 (quotation from p. 425).

2. S. Hord, *Professional Learning Communities: Communities of Continuous Inquiry and Improvement* (Austin, Tex.: SEDL, 1997). www.sedl.org/pubs/catalog/items/cha34.html.

3. M. Collay, D. Dunlap, W. Enloe, and G. Gagnon, *Learning Circles: Creating Conditions for Teacher Professional Development* (Thousand Oaks, Calif.: Corwin Press, 1998).

4. Collay, Dunlap, Enloe, and Gagnon, *Learning Circles*, 1998, p. 2.

5. E. Wenger, *Communities of Practice: Learning, Meaning, and Identity* (London: Cambridge University Press, 1998).

6. Wenger, *Communities of Practice*, 1998, p. 72.

7. D. Johnson and R. Johnson, *Learning Together and Alone* (Englewood Cliffs, N. J.: Prentice Hall, 1983).

8. J. Murphy, *Connecting School Leadership and School Improvement* (Thousand Oaks, Calif.: Corwin Press, 2005).

9. J. Spillane, T. Hallett, and J. Diamond, "Forms of Capital and the Construction of Leadership: Instructional Leadership in Urban Elementary Schools," *Sociology of Education* 76(1) (2003): 1–17.

10. Wenger, *Communities of Practice*, 1998, p. 73.

11. Wenger, *Communities of Practice*, 1998.

12. K. Marshall, *Rethinking Teacher Evaluation: How to Work Smart, Build Collaboration, and Close the Achievement Gap* (San Francisco: Jossey-Bass, 2010).

13. J. Spillane, "Distributed Leadership," *The Educational Forum* 69 (Winter 2005): 143–150.

14. H. Hayes Jacobs, *Mapping the Big Picture: Integrating Curriculum and Assessment* (Alexandria, Va.: ASCD, 1997).

5

INQUIRY IS LEADING

The real act of discovery consists not in finding
new lands but seeing with new eyes.

—*Marcel Proust*

In previous chapters, my colleagues described their beliefs about
leadership for learning with particular emphasis on improving
classroom-based instruction for students. Regular and systematic
work examining their own students' achievement data with colleagues led many to realize that their students' success in the classroom was hindered by inequitable policies and practices that exist
beyond the four walls of the classroom. Teachers "saw with new
eyes" the influence of instructional patterns, curriculum structures, and narrowly framed assessments on their students. When
teachers study their own classroom practice, they change not only
how they teach and learn, but influence their grade or department, school, and district. Action research, inquiry, problem-
based learning, or asking questions about student learning changes
the quality of teacher and student learning every day. Systematic
inquiry can also influence practice far beyond the site.

Regular, systematic inquiry about student learning is an act of
research that moves teaching closer to professional status. Teacher-
led inquiry or action research challenges norms of top-down solutions to age-old problems of schooling. Dana and Yendol-Hoppey[1]
suggest: "Teacher inquiry is a vehicle that can be used by teachers
to untangle some of the complexity that occurs in the profession,
raise teachers' voices in discussions of educational reform, and ultimately transform assumptions about the teaching profession itself.

Transforming the profession is really the capstone to the teacher inquiry story."

Teachers don't need a textbook about inquiry or action research to know there are problems to be studied. Many texts do, however, provide guidelines or structures for teams undertaking research on practice. The first step is recognizing the problem and finding support to take up the work. Some problems are small and can be managed at the site. Others are large and reflect disparities in the larger society. In one elementary school a teacher lamented, "What kind of lesson are we teaching our students when we separate them by level of academic ability? Are we telling them that one class is better than another? Are we telling them that one class is smarter or dumber than the other class?" Her observation is no "discovery" of a single, misguided assessment, but reflects a moral imperative to challenge larger patterns of stratified schooling.

Further examination and heightened awareness of policies and practices at the school, district, state, or federal level have led many teachers to advocate for changes that benefit students, families, and communities. Questioning inequitable practices that affect each roomful of students is a required step towards transforming learning across the school and throughout education. Norms of educational practice are evident in every classroom, school, and district every day. Leaders discover those patterns in their classrooms and are moved to take action outside the four walls. In the next section are some examples of how different leaders have used systematic inquiry to mitigate or change poor or discriminatory practices and transform policies and practices where they are. These examples come from all levels of schooling.

Using Inquiry Where You Are

The classroom is a small school in itself, and, like schools, it reflects many aspects of the larger society. To teach, therefore, is to become a player on the stage of activism by leading educational transformation to support greater access to educational opportunities for all students. Improving learning opportunities for students by challenging policies is a powerful act of leadership. "Leadership means taking responsibility for something you care about."[2] Awareness of what's not working for students starts with teachers in classrooms. Through systematic investigation, teachers capture student experiences and document patterns, then link those patterns to forces outside the grade level, department, and school.

Inquiry About Classrooms as Part of a Larger System

Dawn worked as a bilingual teacher for several years before garnering enough support to challenge de facto tracking of intermediate students: "In the past years, we have had two major programs at the school site, the Gifted and Talented Education program (GATE) and the Bilingual Education program, respectively. Both of these programs allow segregation to occur." This teacher and a couple of her colleagues had observed that bilingual students stayed in the bilingual cohort after they had met the standard to exit the program and were not considered "qualified" for the GATE program. Initially, they sought access for their qualified students to be admitted to that program. The eventual goal was to dismantle the two tracks and create a more integrated program with better resources for all students.

In this next example, a teacher who has worked to improve language acquisition strategies with her own students is taking her work outside the classroom. She has done some legwork and learned about teachers in other schools who are getting similar results. Natalie is resolute in her plan to take her recommendations forward, while anticipating her recommendations might not be heard the first time around: "I plan to meet with our Site-Based Decision-Making Team and present my data and the recommendations that go along with it. From there, I will see what happens. If nothing results, I will try again, for the sake of our disadvantaged students. We need to see what is working in other classrooms, schools, and districts for English language learners and implement those strategies in our classrooms."

Natalie's curriculum expertise positioned her to articulate what was working and what was needed in and beyond her classroom. As a teacher, she didn't assume her recommendations would be accepted immediately, but kept the purpose of serving students at the center of her efforts.

For larger systems to change, educational leadership that emerges in site-based teams must build strength at that level and then be channeled to influence the larger system. Teachers are well positioned to offer leadership within their teams by engaging in research about the problems that arise. They and other leaders can move outside the team and work across the school and beyond to effect change. Systematic inquiry about how things got the way they are lays the foundation for what to do about it.

Inquiry About Curriculum

There's a saying in politics to "follow the dollar," meaning that if we want to know how particular legislation is established and sustained, we need to look at the financial and political underpinnings. What interest groups supported the legislation, what opportunities were provided by that legislation, and who benefited? In schools, we must follow policies that represent political actions. Schools are agents of the state, and changing state and federal policies affect students in classrooms. Teachers seeking answers often need to ask, "What policy or legislation is in play? How does it affect my classroom? What can be done to improve it, disrupt it, or change it?" Teachers see the impact of legislation every day, whether through federal mandates, state-adopted textbooks, or district assessments. Teachers know legislation by the impact on their students, but aren't always positioned to moderate the effects of that legislation.

A useful inquiry is to follow any policy from its legislation through various degrees of implementation. One example of federal legislation is bilingual policy that changes with federal and state elections. Bilingual programs are highly political, and teachers who work in those programs become politicized, whether by choice or circumstance. For instance, many researchers who study second-language acquisition recommend first-language instruction through the early grades or until students are literate in that language. English instruction is gradually added through the grades until middle school, when students are expected to work at grade level in English. Federal legislation like No Child Left Behind or other standardized testing mandates require assessment in English in second grade. This assessment framework pressures teachers and families to use English-only immersion settings for young children who are then tested in a language they haven't yet learned. Special education referrals are much higher for second-language speakers. Those referrals are often based on problematic assessment data, rather than a more comprehensive evaluation.

Teachers bring and develop expertise in specific pedagogy or other areas of work and are excited about sharing that practice. While norms about teachers sharing expertise are often conflicting, many find their specialty being appreciated by others. Tom describes his transition from department-based leadership to the district setting: "This last year I realized my goal of helping teachers become better math instructors. During the school year I was an academic English coach and was able to coach five teachers with those techniques. This summer I was hired by the district to coach four math teachers during summer school. This was an invaluable experience because I was able to influence not only one class of students, but many more by helping teachers use best practices and modeling our math teaching techniques."

Influencing others is a central tenet of leadership action, and the power to influence systems beyond the school is evident in these reflections. Inquiry processes that begin in the classroom have great potential to move outward, changing larger systems from within.

Inquiry About Student Assessment

Standardized assessment of student learning has been taken over by agencies outside the classroom, and while these data are touted by reformers, they have limited use in classrooms. Teachers must "follow the data" those agencies provide while continuing to work inside the classroom and school to retain and strengthen other forms of student and program evaluation. For educational leaders to identify and implement transformative educational practices in classrooms, schools, and districts, they must find, manage, and interpret many kinds of data. Data can be organized in ways that allow greater understanding and usefulness for educators and their clients. Standardized test data are somewhat useful in portraying student achievement, but numeric and demographic data about the school and community, the history of enrollment and staffing, and the politics of the district and board provide additional lenses for inquiry. Hannah, for instance, uses achievement scores and descriptive data to point out the disparity between schools in her district: "Students in poor urban schools are required to perform at the same level as suburban schools. There is a lack of resources for students to reach an understanding of the subject matter. There is a high turnover of teachers within these schools. We have hired twelve new teachers this year. Whenever a staff has a high turnover rate, the consistency that is required in order for students to excel is not there."

Standardized test scores are the primary criteria used to judge school success, so teachers are pressured to use such data exclusive of other essential measures. Low-performing schools lose authority over their curriculum, and many urban school staffs suffer the indignities of punishment for poor performance, even as they strive to respond to mandates that require "standards-based" instruction and related assessments. Niko describes the effect of high-stakes testing in his school: "The format of multiple-choice testing has significant limitations in its structure and implementation, particularly when educators are encouraged at great length to 'teach to the test' and provide extensive test readiness and test preparation. Many students who can correctly bubble in the desired answer from a composed list of choices are frequently unable to create meaningful and in-depth answers when multiple-choice responses are no longer available." Because standardized test scores dominate the landscape, it is essential that teachers develop strong evaluation skills so they can integrate other forms of assessment and present a comprehensive image of students' knowledge.

Teachers observe firsthand every day the negative consequences of ill-conceived federal policies. Many teachers are strategic in protecting their students from the worst effects through individual actions in their classrooms, but find they need to act collectively to change the system. By establishing purposeful, research-based communities of practice in teams and departments, teachers can push back against shortsighted reforms and work over the long term to transform practice. Niko articulates an important foundation of site-based leadership: "When teachers find a professional home and stay in a school and department or team over a longer period of time, we become a powerful resource for our colleagues." In addition to developing efficacy at the site, he is taking his expertise to the district advisory forum: "I participate in the district's Transitional Bilingual English committee and brought up the question of the poor statistics for short-term bilingual programs such as the one at our school and in most of the district schools. The leadership responded that it is highly aware of the problem, but it is disposed to do what it can with what we have now because changing things would be a momentous undertaking."

Many kinds of data can inform leadership in the classroom, school, and beyond. These data are captured through surveys and interviews and can be examined alongside achievement data, demographic data, and teacher characteristics. Qualitative data are essential to understanding the cultural life of a school, including real student work, schoolwide performances, anecdotal stories, community lore, or anything that illuminates the story of one particular classroom, grade level or department, or school. Teachers swim in pools of standardized, norm-referenced achievement data, but more qualitative information can illuminate some of the reasons for those achievement data and must be gathered just as systematically.

Inquiry About the Culture of the School

One approach to more fully understanding the school community is through a school culture audit. A handful of organization assessment processes is available for school leaders' use (see the Resources section at the end of this chapter). Examples include Lambert's leadership capacity surveys, Katzenmeyer's and Moller's teacher inventories, Frost and colleagues' inquiry process for school improvement, and the Equity Audit developed by the Association of California School Administrators (ACSA).[3] Parent leadership materials and district parent surveys can also provide data. An audit allows school leaders to engage their colleagues in collecting and examining their own and colleagues' beliefs. The data create a profile of the organization and how it functions. The ACSA Position Paper and Equity Audit tool articulates essential dimensions of a healthy school. Administering an audit provokes lots of discussion and provides a container for data gathering.

While such surveys are often used as a measure to establish a baseline, the discussions about their use and purpose, who should be surveyed, and when and how the data will be reviewed are another form of measuring how the community is functioning. What my colleagues found about their schools when they administered the audit was multilayered. Asking their peers to engage with the survey was as instructive as the data itself.

One teacher described how her colleagues reacted when she introduced the concept of an audit.

Mary, a Latina teaching in her home neighborhood, recalled that earlier in the year she had asked "my entire staff if they would please fill out the questionnaire to the best of their abilities." She explained the purpose was to "get a general feeling from the staff about how equitable the education system was at our school site." Her colleagues were suspicious. "Immediately I was being challenged by many of my colleagues as to the purpose and who was going to see the results." She tried to assure them the findings would be confidential, but the process did not go smoothly:

> After the staff meeting that day, I placed the questionnaires in their mailboxes. Once many staff members read through the questionnaire, they asked again why they had to put their names on the questionnaire and who was going to see it. To ease tension, I said that I would shred the documents once I gathered the information that I needed and that if they felt better, I did not need their names. It was so I could see the differences of opinions by grade level, gender, race, and age. After answering many similar questions I received twenty-seven of the thirty-one questionnaires that I sent out.

One purpose of the ACSA Equity Audit is to capture the different ways teachers, students, and families experience school. The audit is intended to help school leaders capture community and teacher perceptions and identify gaps and limitations in the areas of curriculum and instruction, assessment, professional learning, and community engagement. If colleagues haven't engaged in regular reflection and evaluation of the quality of education across their sites, the audit process jump-starts the conversation. It can also create tension and make people defensive about whether or to what degree they are serving students and families. Some teachers may feel unfairly judged by the process of being surveyed. Mary continues her story about administering the Equity Audit:

> After carefully reviewing and tallying up answers, I noticed that many of my colleagues felt that there were no inequities at my school site. I thought this unrealistic and went to a trusted colleague and asked her why that might be the case. While my colleagues are good people and we believe they intended to assist me in any way possible, they continued to have apprehensions about filling out the surveys. Due to the uneasiness, it is quite possible that a handful of my coworkers answered the survey so it would not affect them in a negative way, should these questionnaires fall into the wrong hands.

I found her reflection disconcerting and yet predictable. Concerns about survey findings "falling into the wrong hands" indicate that some of Mary's colleagues did not trust the process. Some may have assumed she was representing the site or a district. Asking for names on the surveys points out her lack of awareness of distrust by teachers. Teachers seldom have the safety to engage in serious conversation about the organization, membership within it, or their own gifts and challenges. Without a strong foundation of trust, few will point out areas where they feel inadequate.[4]

Carrying an audit into a school does not lead directly to school improvement. Asking the right questions in a respectful way must be at the heart of any inquiry, and taking up difficult matters without incorporating confidentiality and other safeguards into the process will not establish trust. In a national reform climate of punishment of the guilty and reward of the victorious, taking action by seeking schoolwide data is a sensitive issue. Teachers make judgments every day about how, when, and with whom to collaborate. Taking up important concerns with the larger community requires the same consideration.

Using Inquiry to Cross Boundaries

When district leaders implement reforms, they are generally responding to state or federal policies that must be implemented in classrooms. Yet the processes required to implement mandates are "loosely coupled"—there are few direct routes from mandate to classroom. Teachers are critical of top-down mandates with good reason. District leaders who seek real change must work with teachers as partners in reform—not just those teachers who appear willing and able to go along with the latest fad, but all teachers, especially those who have seen mandates, superintendents, and illogical reforms come and go. Teachers are mediators of reform, not mere recipients of instructions to do more or less of something. Some reform literature contains language such as teacher "buy-in," "motivation," and "resistance." Such language is patronizing and reinforces the management-labor relationship of teachers with others, makes teachers the problem, and does not imagine a professional framework in which useful change is encouraged. Teacher-led inquiry may begin in the classroom, but it soon leads to asking questions about the organization, systems, and policies beyond the district.

Inquiry About Professional Development

Renee is a middle-school teacher who leads within and beyond her school by researching curricular approaches, building her expertise in her classroom, and exchanging ideas with others. As a team member who has developed a specialty in one area of instruction, she is confident about sharing that expertise in-house and throughout the district. She describes moving her expertise outward from her school into the district: "Aside from developing these units for my class as curriculum leader, I have shared many of the strategies with my colleagues across the district. This allowed me to create meaningful professional relationships with my peers, so we can interact to ensure that students are receiving a variety of instructional practices to enhance their educational experience."

Renee works on a regular basis with teachers at other schools, establishing a "ground-up" response to student learning, rather than a top-down, policy-driven approach. Her curriculum design has improved the quality of instruction that her students and their counterparts receive at this school and other schools. Her leadership is influencing districtwide policy through her contribution to developing the district's master plan:

> This year I have been involved in the development of the English Language Learners' Master Plan, as well as aligning and mapping the sixth-grade course content with the other two middle schools. Both of these tasks have required a lot of collaboration time with teachers at my site and the other two middle schools. I feel that these opportunities have really allowed me to learn how to delegate and lead tasks that need to be done at my site and how to compromise with others to create one coherent piece of work that reflects the whole middle school community.

Educational leadership requires keeping student learning front and center, and student learning is organized and led by teachers in classrooms. Teacher expertise is planted there, and seeds from those labors can be sown in other fields, creating transformation from the ground up. In the next excerpt, Nanette, a teacher on special assignment (TOSA) discusses teaching all subject areas to English language learners. Through site-based inquiry and study, she has developed facilitation skills that support professional development at her school, and she questions the efficacy of centralized training and the mandate driving it:

> Although I feel that coaching is a valuable tool, our district is spending too much money to send people to training when the information is never disseminated to schools where it would make the difference. The district would be better off sending

grade-level teams, making them the experts. All of this comes back to one thing: teachers need training, and students need time to learn and become proficient in a second language. No Child Left Behind states that all students will be reading by the third grade. What provisions is the government making for a student learning a new language beginning in second or third grade? The answer is none. I believe that the system is flawed, not the schools.

As a school-based coach, Nanette believes that her on-site approach to professional development is more effective than centralized training of individual teachers in response to a mandate. She furthermore believes that mandating students to read in English by a certain age does not help newcomers become proficient. Her capacity to structure English language curriculum is essential to her colleagues, but that knowledge in and of itself is not a fix without attending to the larger political context. This important dimension of leadership leads to the next area of teacher inquiry: asking questions about mandates and policies.

Inquiry About Mandates and Policies

English language curriculum and assessment are especially political, and teachers find themselves guardians of the gate in multiple ways. Debates about how other languages should be used or taught take place every day in many schools throughout the country. Shifting accountability policies present educational leaders with constant challenges, yet offer points of leverage for teachers who seek to mitigate the most onerous outcomes and strengthen those policies that are most effective. Between Race to the Top, No Child Left Behind, and the reforms that preceded them, contemporary school leaders are awash in federal mandates, regulations, and case law. To lead educational transformation on any level, educational leaders must know some history and intention of policies and mandates. Teachers understand the experiences of the student in relation to those mandates, particularly those experiences that are invisible to policymakers. Decision making about actions can then be informed by the intent of the policy and real experiences.

Teachers strive to teach effectively in spite of poorly conceived mandates, not with the aid of such mandates. Teaching well within a culture of mandated reform forces teachers to challenge those bureaucratic constraints every day if they want to succeed in the classroom. Questions must be asked, data collected, and decisions made in response to those data. School site leaders sometimes characterize teacher interrogation of the latest mandate as "resistance." The description is apt, perhaps, when teachers resist ill-conceived policies and mandates that punish the inhabitants of schools while not changing schools for the better.

Inquiry About the Community

Bobbie is a young teacher in a neighborhood high school that is invisible to most of the community. Bobbie worked closely with a few media artists near her school to research and implement a project-based media design curriculum. She has successfully engaged marginalized young people in productive academic work through her outreach to the local community and must now find ways to convince district-level leaders about her vision: "One of the hardest things for a school to do is get the community and district to support the vision of the school, especially when they both seem so unsupportive."

Adjacent to one of the largest seaports in the country, the African American neighborhood has changed over recent decades from an industrial working-class enclave to a gentrified commuter neighborhood. Bobbie was raised in the neighborhood and brings to her team local knowledge of the neighbors and their stories. She describes her ongoing efforts to understand the history and culture of the community and to improve the school's visibility: "Our high school continues to bring itself into the community, making our vision for our students well known to the people who walk by every day. Students are required to do community service both on and off campus; community members are constantly brought in to classrooms as inspirational speakers or to teach lessons. Nearby organizations and community professionals are used as partners in school programs, and local businesses are engaged in our work."

Teachers, especially those in immigrant and poor communities, often find themselves crucial mediators for newcomers or marginalized mainstream culture. Rosanna was raised in a Spanish-speaking neighborhood and now works in a Latino newcomer community and reaches out to the parents of her elementary school–age students. She identified the high rate of Latino dropout as a civil rights issue. In this excerpt, Rosanna recalls the story of her older sister:

My sister dropped out when she was in the eleventh grade because high school was boring. She refused to go to school and started to work instead. She didn't have to work; she chose to work. I was in the tenth grade at the time, and I remember thinking nothing of it. My mother and father did not give her a hard time about it either. They told her that if she wasn't going to school, then she would have to work. I remember her being a lot happier working than being in school. She didn't have a drug problem, she wasn't pregnant, she wasn't in a gang, and she wasn't below grade level. She was an average student. No one at our high school did anything about it. None of her six teachers called to find out why she had dropped out of school. Sadly, neither her counselor nor principal took three minutes of their day to call to see what was going on. I guess they were used to seeing students drop out. This story is probably similar to the story of many other Latinos.

Rosanna is driven by the inequities her own family experienced to provide greater resources for her students. Her leadership in the school community is powerfully informed by her upbringing in a situation similar to theirs. Another teacher who draws on local knowledge, she acts as a mediator, a translator, and a guide for parents who are not able to advocate for their children. So often, teachers act as cross-cultural mediators in the ways Bobbie and Rosanna do. Their rich knowledge about their communities is directed to changing policies and practices and offer other teachers a vital example of inquiry.

When teachers make choices about how to teach content, the cultural setting of the school can and should become the context for learning. In one school, fifth-grade teachers structured an immigration unit around U.S. history curriculum standards. Students were assigned the task of interviewing an immigrant and learning about their experiences when coming to the United States. An elderly Japanese woman who had been interned in a camp during World War II was a guest presenter. In another school, a third-grade teacher took her students through the local Chinatown, where some students acted as interpreters and tour guides, introducing family establishments and elders in the community. A high school science class visited a local media animation company, Pixar, to learn how movie developers set up storyboards with old-fashioned felt before moving onto computers to design characters.

As noted earlier, teachers come to the work of classroom teaching from all walks of life, with wide-ranging values, varying beliefs about how to conduct the work, and different goals and professional aspirations. Teachers come to the work of classroom teaching enabled by support systems to do work and use those same networks to strengthen teaching. "It takes a village" may seem a bit shopworn since the time Hilary Clinton took the adage into the mainstream, but there is truth in the notion that many people educate a child. School staff members are an important part of a child's life and a community's life. In some communities, the school is at the center—witness the grief when a school closes, whether on the prairie or in a bankrupt urban district. For other communities, going to the school is a risky proposition, as Immigration and Naturalization Services (INS) agents could turn up and demand proof of citizenship.

In Chapter Four, we looked at the ways teachers carry expertise in teaching and learning beyond individual classrooms and to different levels of the school. The approaches described began with classroom-based expertise and flowed outward. As you strive to work more systematically with others in a more concerted way, it is essential to understand how organizations function and how they might function better. The Equity Plan presented in Inquiry Five later in this chapter is designed to support teachers in managing systems and strengthening organizational structures in schools. Four faculty members in an educational leadership program collaborated to design this approach to identifying inequities in schooling practices.[5] The inquiry is structured to support school leaders in naming, reframing, and addressing systemic inequity.

Considerations About Inquiry as Leading

- Complex problems require complex solutions; maintain a healthy skepticism when you are offered a simple solution to a challenging problem.
- Trust your instincts and ask a lot of questions on behalf of your community members (students, families, and sometimes colleagues).
- Strive to refine and articulate your inquiry. What is the problem, and who can help you address it?
- Gather obvious data first, but extend your thinking and your reach into other kinds of information that can shed light on your dilemmas or your colleagues' perplexities.
- Reach across roles and boundaries to enlist allies in your effort.
- Take your initial findings to a sympathetic audience and garner their support in strengthening your points and building your argument.

- If you can't find the information or data to help you address your inquiry, it may not exist in the form you need. Get help—and get different data by creating or revising existing tools.

- Revisit the kinds of data and information you do have with new eyes. Standardized test scores tell us some things about students' knowledge, but the information is limited and can't capture the whole story of what happened in your classroom or school this year.

- Align standardized test scores with other sources of information about student learning to create a comprehensive picture of what students know and how they express what they know.

- Use authentic assessment approaches from existing sources to ground your inquiry, and provide varied, student-created materials for evaluation.

❧ INQUIRY FIVE ❧
Framework for Developing an Equity Plan

The power of facilitating any inquiry work comes from a question or concern from your own classroom. Equity plans are teacher-led, focus on students and systems, and support change in the larger unit of the school, district, or region. Taking your questions or observations through a collaborative process like the Equity Plan (or other cycles of inquiry you may be familiar with) extends your advocacy beyond your immediate class or department.

At the classroom level, you make observations and judgments about individual students, including how they relate to specific materials, peers, and school in general. As you work in role-alike groups and cross-role groups, you may see similar patterns or anomalies. Colleagues may share similar concerns, parents may ask you about procedures, or other leaders may seek your advice. Your own professional development activities beyond the school provide additional perspectives on why things are the way they are. Your everyday planning, implementing, and modification of instruction are the centerpiece of your leadership. In doing the work of designing curriculum, you will see larger systemic problems beyond the classroom that profoundly affect student learning inside your classroom, grade level, department, and school. There are many well-wrought classroom inquiry protocols to choose from; see the Resources list later in this chapter for help identifying the ones that will work best in your setting. Use the outline below for brainstorming, planning, and organizing materials.

Question or Concern

- Identify an area of student learning that you wish to study. Gather student work or standardized data that led you to your question.

- With a partner or small team, discuss your question or concern and identify sources of information that can inform your inquiry. The sources can include site historians (colleagues who have background information), program implementation efforts, state or federal mandates, assessments, or survey findings.

Data Analysis

- What kinds of data are available? Use student, school, and district benchmark tests; assessment material from tools embedded in curriculum; portfolios; grades; failure rates; or survey data from parents. Why did you choose to look at these particular sources of data?

- Analyze these data: What does the information tell you? What is not evident in the information you have? What additional information would be useful? What trends or patterns do you see? What are the equity concerns? (Does the information or data reflect demographic characteristics of students?)

- Go outside the "data box" and identify any informal, anecdotal, or survey student data you have, such as focus group data, informal conversations with students, student surveys, accreditation data, and attendance. How do these data relate to the student achievement data? What are the equity implications?

- Use a school culture audit tool and self-study survey material to learn more about teacher, staff, and parent perspectives.[6] What do these data tell you? How does this relate to what you see in the student achievement data? What are the equity implications? Are there additional data you would like to have? If so, what are they, and why would they be useful?

- Now that you have analyzed the data and information, what is the equity problem that you address with your plan? Why did you choose this focus?

Collaboration

- Describe your partner or team. Why did you choose this person or group?
- What is the relationship of this person or group to the focus of your inquiry? Who else can support your effort?
- What additional insights did you get as a result of your collaboration? How will this partnership serve the students?

Actions and Resources

- Identify existing resources and those that may be needed to support your goals for equitable outcomes.
- Consider how resources might be aligned to create greater equity for students.
- Identify district-level trends or external policies that might support or limit your efficacy.

Recommendations

- Your recommendations should span an academic year and grow from the findings from your data analysis and collaboration. They should be specific and detailed and may include collecting additional data.
- Describe and explain each recommendation. Why is each one included among your recommendations? How does it relate to the data? How will you go about implementing it? Who will be involved? What is the anticipated outcome? How will it address the basic equity problem you have identified?
- What next steps do you anticipate once you have implemented your plan—further data collection, further collaboration, or others?

Resources

Association of California School Administrators, "Position Paper and Equity Audit," 2005.
www.acsa.org.

This organization provides resources specific to the principalship and other certified administrative roles that focus on teaching, learning, equity, and advocacy. The web site offers educational leadership resources such as the school equity position paper. The site is geared for members, but some materials such as the Equity Audit are available to everyone.

Dana, N., and Yendol-Hoppey, D., *Reflective Educators' Guide to Classroom Research: Learning to Teach and Teaching to Learn Through Practitioner Inquiry*, 2nd ed. (Thousand Oaks, Calif.: Corwin Press, 2009).

This is a step-by-step guide for teachers and others doing classroom-based inquiry. The rationale for teacher inquiry is useful from a professional development perspective, with attention to developing questions, situating the work, structuring collaboration, and writing up the work.

Frost, D., Durrant, J., Head, M., and Holden, G., *Teacher-Led School Improvement* (New York: RoutledgeFalmer, 2000).

Frost and his coauthors describe the ways teachers in the United Kingdom needed to "rebuild teacher professionalism" in the face of nationalizing the curriculum. The authors and participants recognize the many leadership roles that teachers play and the importance of teacher expertise in the midst of reform. The section on uses of teacher-led inquiry is especially useful.

Gagnon, G., and Collay, M., *Constructivist Learning Design: Key Questions for Teaching to Standards* (Thousand Oaks, Calif.: Corwin Press, 2006).

This text grew out of our collaboration with teachers who were using constructivist approaches in lesson design.

Our goals were to create a framework for more systematic documentation of work that teachers were already doing and to demonstrate how constructivist teaching and learning could support interpretation and implementation of curriculum standards.

Katzenmeyer, M., and Moller, G., *Awakening the Sleeping Giant: Helping Teachers Develop as Leaders*, 3rd ed. (Thousand Oaks, Calif.: Corwin Press, 2009).

Now in its third edition, this text continues serve a broad range of teacher leadership audiences. The authors give well-researched definitions of teacher leadership, offer a range of self-study and facilitator-friendly activities, and stay grounded in the real world of school reform. As one reviewer noted, the authors have stayed abreast of the evolving world of teacher leadership.

Lambert, L., *Leadership Capacity for Lasting School Improvement* (Alexandria, Va.: ASCD, 2003).

Lambert's books about school leadership provide a succinct and accessible framework for practitioners leading school change. She has framed the work of school leadership around leadership actions, rather than assigning leadership tasks to conventional roles. The assessment and survey tools that accompany the text are very useful for gathering information, provoking conversation, and supporting change.

Mueller, J., "Authentic Assessment Toolbox," (2010). http://jonathan.mueller.faculty.noctrl.edu/toolbox/tasks.htm.

This web site offers educators a primer on "authentic assessment," a comprehensive approach to documenting and evaluating not only what students know, but how they can apply that knowledge. Authentic assessment is not new, but the pressures of accountability have marginalized this important work. New and experienced teachers alike will find the information relevant and useful.

National Equity Project (formerly BayCES).
www.bayces.org.

The National Equity Project is a nonprofit organization based in Oakland, California, whose mission is leadership development with a particular emphasis on creating equitable conditions in urban schools. The senior leadership team and school-based coaches have decades of experience as classroom teachers, coaches, policy developers, and partners in a range of districts throughout the country. Coaching resources are available.

National Writing Project.
www.nwp.org/cs/public/print/doc/about.csp.

Established by and for teachers in the 1970s, the National Writing Project is now the intellectual home for thousands of teachers who attend summer institutes to develop their own writing skills, learn about teaching writing, implement powerful writing instruction, and establish and conduct their own research on the writing process. Over two hundred regional projects offer sustained professional support for teachers from many disciplines and educational levels.

Schmuck, R., *Practical Action Research for Change,* 2nd ed. (Thousand Oaks, Calif.: Corwin Press, 2006).

Action research is a tried-and-true form of collaborative study that is performed in the context of other professional work. The author outlines steps toward a collaborative inquiry process and offers examples of teacher teams and their inquiry efforts. This tradition is particularly helpful for those working across roles, such as teachers and parents or other community members.

Notes

The epigraph to this chapter is drawn from M. Proust, À la recherche du temps perdu (In Search of Lost Time, also translated as Remembrance of Things Past), (Paris: Bernard Grasse, 1913–1927).

1. N. Dana and D. Yendol-Hoppey, *Reflective Educators' Guide to Classroom Research: Learning to Teach and Teaching to Learn Through Practitioner Inquiry* (Thousand Oaks, Calif.: Corwin Press, 2009).
2. S. Jubb, personal communication, August 2001.
3. L. Lambert, *Leadership Capacity for Lasting School Improvement* (Alexandria, Va.: ASCD, 2003); M. Katzenmeyer and G. Moller, *Awakening the Sleeping Giant: Helping Teachers Develop as Leaders* (Thousand Oaks, Calif.: Corwin Press, 2001); D. Frost, J. Durrant, M. Head, and G. Holden, *Teacher-Led School Improvement* (New York: RoutledgeFalmer, 2000); Association of California School Administrators, "Position Paper and Equity Audit," 2005. www.acsa.org.
4. A. Bryk and B. Schneider, *Trust in Schools: A Core Resource for School Improvement* (New York: Russell Sage Foundation, 2002).
5. M. Collay, P. Winkelman, R. Garcia, and J. Guilkey-Amado, "Transformational Leadership Pedagogy: Implementing Equity Plans in Urban Schools," *Educational Leadership and Administration* (in press).
6. Association of California School Administrators, "Position Paper and Equity Audit," 2005; Lambert, *Leadership Capacity*, 2003; Katzenmeyer and Moller, *Awakening the Sleeping Giant*, 2001.

6

PARTNERSHIP IS LEADING

Schooling is what happens inside the walls of the
school, some of which is educational. Education
happens everywhere, and it happens from the
moment a child is born—and some people say
before—until a person dies.

—*Sara Lawrence Lightfoot*

In Chapter One, I presented a brief history of school leadership,
setting the backdrop for reframing classroom teaching as leadership. In subsequent chapters, my colleagues and I offered our
thinking about leadership for learning from the inside out. As
teachers and students run the curricular course together, learning happens. Whether that learning is schooling or education
is the province of the teacher. Each teacher's life history, values,
and sense of the role provide a foundation upon which the classroom experience is imagined and structured. The classroom setting is the container: it sometimes buffers schooling and allows
learning and at other times frees the students to be led outward,
to be educated.

Schooling, as Lightfoot suggests, occurs when teachers feel
limited by the four walls of the classroom. *Taking action from the
classroom out* places the teacher and students at the center of
the cell: they are the DNA of the larger body of the community
and the world. As effective school leaders, teachers lead in the
classroom, school, and community every day. Interacting across
each of these settings, resourceful teachers lead for transformation, rather than reproduction, of existing practice and seek to

transform, not reproduce, policies and practices that limit educational access and opportunities for so many students.

Transformative leaders have the following values, or four "I"s: idealized charisma or influence, inspirational motivation, intellectual stimulation, and individualized consideration.[1] These characteristics are evident in strong leaders at all levels of an organization. Visionary leaders strive to develop and sustain transformational organizations or learning organizations that reflect the purposes and goals of their membership. Schools are organizations populated by teachers and students who have not designed them, however, so the journey is uphill and the path is rocky. In spite of the intractable social challenges that schools are ill designed to address, many teachers succeed in improving their school's capacity to educate. Fortunately, organizations can be transformed—even schools. While teachers do not always feel well positioned to effect change, they are our last, best hope. According to Senge: "Learning organizations are where people continually expand their capacity to create the results they truly desire, where new and expansive patterns of thinking are nurtured, where collective aspiration is set free, and where people are continually learning to see the whole together."[2]

Teachers can and do "expand their capacity to create results they truly desire" when it comes to enacting more and better learning options for students. When teachers gain experience and "see the whole together," it becomes clear that larger, systemic problems emanate from beyond classroom walls. While some challenges limiting student success in the classroom are societal, others are embedded in schooling itself. Sustained change that transforms classroom learning therefore requires leading change in all parts of the organization. Teachers must bring a teaching-and-learning stance into other dimensions of the organization to create schools that are true learning organizations. Part of the work of organizational change is knowing how change happens (or doesn't happen) and applying change theory every day.[3] Focusing on the school or district as the

unit of analysis without recognizing teachers as leaders reinforces use of bureaucratic, top-down strategies. We know these
approaches don't work.

Organizations change because courageous individuals take a
stand. Teachers are closest to the clients, so they are in the best
position to advocate for students and families. Developing the
countenance of a change agent while maintaining membership in
a staff isn't easy. Fran is a mid-career fifth-grade teacher who is just
finding her voice as a leader. She states: "I believe my challenge is
having confidence in myself. I need to speak out when I see problems and inequities and not be a passive bystander." Teaching
is not a role that evokes images of passive bystanders, yet
the machinery that drives schooling can thwart initiative from
even the most stalwart leader.

Fran captures the tensions many teachers feel: "It may be
easier to bury myself with my own students and not worry about
what goes on outside of my classroom walls, but it would not be
fair to our school's students, nor our staff and community. It is
something I must work on every day if I want to be an effective
leader in my classroom, school, and community." These words
capture the essence of the classroom as a microcosm of a larger
world, and an essential part of educational leadership is making connections to other individuals, agencies, and organizations. Partnering with others can be the force that makes action
possible.

In this final chapter, I review the work of teachers in partnership with organizations and agencies beyond the classroom.
Teachers draw strength and expertise from partnerships and use
knowledge gained in those partnerships to influence how school
and district representatives respond to students, families, and
communities. Within those agencies and organizations, teachers find like-minded souls who can walk alongside them on their
journey. The first step on the path to establishing partnerships
beyond the classroom is recognition of the school or district as
a collection of individuals. How often do we hear "the school

says" or "the school does" this or that? While the school is not a human being, we often speak of the organization of "school" as speaking or doing. The *school*, whether in our neighborhood or across town, is an agent in the lives of families and communities. And while the school represents the district and state, teachers are the actors that bring the script to life.

District Partnerships

Children and families live in neighborhoods and communities and interact primarily with the neighborhood school or their school of choice, not the district or regional agencies. As teachers and families, we do reside in school districts, but the actions of the larger agency are invisible to us most of the time. When I drop off my child at school in the morning, I talk to teachers, office-based staff, and other parents. Seldom do I interact with central office–based individuals. "My school," with those specific teachers, staff, and parents, is part of my neighborhood and my community. Many teachers have similar experiences. Their professional home is the school, not the district, and building bridges to that bureaucracy can be complicated and discouraging. Knowing when, how, and with whom to connect with at the larger agency makes it possible for teachers to advocate for students and families. Developing relationships with individuals at the district is an essential requirement for school leadership.

Let me offer a metaphor for how teachers generally experience external mandates and policies that shape their world, and then propose some alternatives. Imagine a conveyor belt positioned outside the school office. Each week, reams of materials are dropped onto the floor. One day the belt carries assessment materials from the district office. Another day it carries federal forms that must be completed for all identified special education students. A third day it carries training materials for the most recent textbook adoption. Much like Lucy Ricardo in the iconic candy-making scene where too many chocolates come off the conveyor belt too quickly to be boxed, teachers soon lose the race against time and material. The piles move through the office into classrooms with little consideration by policymakers of how their use will support or disrupt student learning. Teachers are sent reams of materials to administer and forms to complete and must decide every day how, when, and with whom to use them.

District leaders are required to broker student services from state and federal agencies, passing the policies, paperwork, and punishment along to principals and teachers who must then mediate those services. Even the most astute principal can't always manage the scope of the work and accurately assess the degree of compliance needed. Providing the right services to the client and aligning the resources to the budget is a huge task. So much uninvited and badly framed material comes into schools, it's a wonder any learning happens at all. These materials morph from year to year, so even experienced teachers are unsure of the relevance and connection of such materials to students' day-to-day learning. Every day teachers consider, analyze, sift through, and broker policies, procedures, and print. Those tasks are large and unending. The erratic delivery of materials lends credence to teacher beliefs that they are unplanned and not really intended to support children's learning. Mediating mandates and materials, even those that have potential to leverage student achievement, requires tremendous fortitude. More important, such management requires care and concern for the end-user, the student.

For those district-level decisions that affect students directly, it's easier to know what action to take. In this first example, middle school English teachers work to implement a language arts curriculum across several schools. Mona, an early years bilingual middle school teacher reported: "I have grown in my professional life through the development of frameworks and program structures at the district level. This year I supported the development of the English Language Learners Master Plan, as well as aligning and mapping the sixth-grade course content with the other two middle schools." The project was deemed worthy partly because of the direct impact on students in this teacher's classroom.

In the next example, district managers made decisions about bus routing that may not have been visible to teachers had the families not brought their concerns to their teachers. Lisette, an immigrant, grandmother, and emerging parent activist, describes taking parents to the district office to lobby for services. "I advocated for adequate transportation after parents came to my classroom to ask me to translate the letters they received from the district office telling them that the routes their children were supposed to take had been canceled." District leaders responded to this teacher and these families as clients, not as numbers in a report.

My mentor Phil Runkel used to say, "Institutions don't act, people do!" Unfortunately, attributing the school or district with action is a fair characterization. We don't "talk" to the district, but we do talk to representatives who may not have the authority to help us solve our problem. District-office colleagues are generally acting as agents of the state or the federal government. Some don't believe they have the authority to change unfair policies or push back against passing mandates. Teachers don't have relationships with the entity, but with individuals within the district office. Within these relationships lies potential to advocate for students and families at the site and to create larger organizational change. Relationships with individual actors must be pursued on behalf of students.

I reviewed Lambert's assumptions of leadership in Chapter One, focusing on her point that "educators are purposeful."[4] In addition to those characteristics, she outlines these three goals of leadership capacity:

1. Develop all adults within the school community—teachers, staff, parents, and community members—as reflective, skillful leaders

2. Achieve steady and lasting improvement in student performance and development

3. Construct schools and districts that are sustainable organizations

Effective teachers are reflective, skillful leaders and perceive their primary role as instructors responsible for student achievement. The everyday work of schools is to ensure that students learn and teachers create the conditions for students to learn. Students and teachers cannot be productive in dysfunctional organizations. All of Lambert's goals are the province of teachers, therefore, including the third one. Teachers who are transformative leaders create or construct schools that are sustainable organizations. Schools that function well are that way because of the individuals who work there. District-level policies and practices certainly can support or hinder school site operations, and all schools suffer from malfunctions in the central office. But if teachers wait for their district-level leaders to provide solutions to their problems, they will wait a long time. Many solutions are in the hands of teachers who must pressure the systems around them to serve the client. Well-functioning districts have a culture that recognizes and draws from teacher expertise and supports authentic governance structures.

Enacting Existing Policies

A key leadership stance that teachers take every day is identifying existing policies that intend to serve student learning or protect their rights and mediating those policies to ensure they do what they were intended to do. In this first example, two middle school teachers realized the policy requiring second-language English students be redesignated in a timely way was not in effect at their site. They state: "Our goal is to identify students who are competent in English and exit them from the support program before entering high school." They note the target students have high test scores and are not receiving additional services, but have not been reclassified as proficient in English. They took action to more fully implement the existing reclassification procedure, as Anita described:

> Our position relates directly to the history of education. As educators, we have many roles. We also need to keep in mind our legal obligations. In 1974, the Chacon-Moscone Bilingual-Bicultural Education Act established transitional bilingual education programs to meet the needs of limited-English-proficient students. Programs such as these inform us of the legal requirements that ensure we are providing equitable outcomes for our students. We need to follow federal guidelines to help identify, provide program placement, and reclassify students as fluent-English-proficient. Due to this law, we chose to create a more convenient way for teachers to move through this process.

This pair worked with their site and district leadership to put redesignation procedures in place at each school and then monitored the use of the protocol until it became normal practice.

In the next example, co-chairs of the English Department led a schoolwide effort to first study and then improve the college-going culture at their high school. They surveyed students regarding their perceptions about attending college and how they would prepare to do so. Moira is a midthirties high school teacher currently serving as department chair. She recalled: "In looking at the cumulative data from the surveys, I discovered that most of my 'regular' freshmen were somewhat sure that they wanted to apply to college; however, they did not intend to meet the requirements needed to get into a two- or four-year college or university. I also noticed that the majority of my AVID students were planning to take the SAT and the ACT tests, while my 'regular' students were mostly unsure about taking these tests."

In this case, the Advancement via Individual Determination (AVID) program offered students support, but it wasn't available to all students. AVID is one of many programs designed to address the systematic diversion of minority students away from college prep coursework. AVID staff provides resources and advocates for students and families with little knowledge about what it takes to go to college. This team used their survey data to engage the teacher leadership team at their high school by raising awareness about tracking at their school. They recognized that AVID and other similar programs provided an important avenue for first-generation college-attending students and worked with their colleagues to embed similar strategies for "regular" students.

Aligning Professional Development with Mandates

Teacher-led professional development in response to mandated change can also be productive and meaningful. Teachers who understand the intent of a policy or curriculum approach and have brokered that work effectively make a path for others to follow. Well-regarded colleagues are much more credible than state- or district-based representatives sent out to the school with the latest curriculum adoption or mandate in a box. Organizational change theory tells us that top-down mandates are not effective—and in education, many of the mandates pushed into districts and schools are not based on knowledge about teaching and learning, but on political trends.

In the next example, Andrea and her team created teacher mentorship teams to support improvement in language instruction. Here, "program improvement" means this school must improve achievement for identified students or be closed or reconstituted. Andrea describes the context of their leadership this way: "We are a program improvement site and district, so we need to change. Reflection on our practice is vital to our future. Therefore, our work seems to be even more meaningful to us as well as to other teachers. . . . It also seems clear they expect our research project to serve as a catalyst to improve school efficacy at our site."

The stakes are high, and this leader portrays her colleagues as motivated by external pressures to change instructional practice. No Child Left Behind or Race to the Top won't change schooling directly, but competent leaders in schools can respond to stated goals in thoughtful ways. Classroom-based leaders can leverage external pressures to improve teaching and learning for students, rather than blaming the faceless bureaucracy for the ills of schooling.

Agency Partnerships

Teachers and other school leaders build relationships with nonprofit and other agencies for personal and professional reasons. Personal reasons can vary from maintaining connections to previous professional settings to newly developed community-based services. Professional reasons to partner include intellectual interest, developing curriculum expertise, accessing resources, or making connections to community leaders who have expertise or political connections. Some teachers find their membership in professional organizations essential to their survival, and their affiliation with those organizations is central to their professional identity. Others reach out to different sources for different kinds of support, behaving more like renaissance women and men. In all cases, partnering effectively is a form of leadership.

Teacher-led professional development often begins with one teacher following his own intellectual pursuits, sharing that passion with students and colleagues, and then becoming an expert resource for students, the school, district, and community. Curriculum design is an essential part of educational leadership. Following are some examples of teachers who lead through curriculum expertise. In these examples, agencies or partnerships between organizations are the resource.

Developing Programs

Irene is an experienced fifth-grade teacher who has taught social studies and English language arts for fifteen years. The social studies curriculum includes American colonial history, and this teacher followed a path from the basic information offered in the state-adopted textbook to designing a rich, intellectually stimulating experience for herself and her students. She recalled "learning about the History Project from a colleague at our school." Irene quickly distinguished the quality of learning in this teacher-led, intellectually powerful setting from more simplistic approaches: "I went to a related literacy institute with some cynicism about teacher workshops as being 'make and take.'"

After finding the History Project an authoritative resource for her own classroom-based instruction, she began to carry her students' work back to the project. Irene describes the evolution of her engagement with other colleagues by saying: "I started putting the kids' work out there. It was exciting to be valued. We were all teachers in the classroom—we were creating this work. The workshops weren't more than ten or fifteen people, but those colleagues questioned your work." This "community of practice" provided a forum for this teacher and others to think together about teaching history and guiding student thinking.

Irene reiterated professional discussions that focused on the question, How were we looking at kids as thinkers? That work is systematic and ongoing, as she noted: "I do two or three workshops a year. Once you start doing this and you're with people who have the interest, there's some impatience with people who aren't interested." Her leadership in curriculum development and instructional approaches was appreciated by her principal, who supported her efforts. Her principal "also brought district people in to see us, which validated us and our work." One teacher's quest to engage her classroom of students in the study of history has influenced the school, the district, and teachers throughout the state.

Another teacher-led curriculum and assessment enterprise is the National Writing Project (NWP). Established by and for teachers in the 1970s, the NWP is now the intellectual home for thousands of teachers who attend summer institutes to develop their own writing skills, learn about teaching writing, implement powerful writing instruction, and establish and conduct their own research on the writing process. At a recent Local Site Research Initiative event, teams of teachers from different regions around the country convened with program staff to share research projects and design data-gathering processes.

A third type of agency support comes from a regional office. Tom, a math department chair at a middle school, reported that his affiliation with the local university and the county office of education had been an important part of his professional development. His goal to increase student achievement was strongly supported by "the co-director of the mathematics professional development project and the Strategic and Intensive Mathematics Initiative." Tom related that "the partnership between experts in the field and teachers in the classroom has been positive and rewarding both for teachers and students. I have become a better math teacher due to this support and partnership. The co-director's personal attention and expertise has encouraged me to take on the role of math department head and teacher leader at my school this year."

Creating Collaboratives

In other cases, teachers create their own structures to support personal and professional development. The next example of teacher collaboration to improve classroom practice comes from mathematics educators. In one middle school in a large district, teachers interested in improving their skills in middle school math instruction met monthly for several years to review lessons, plan instruction, set up observations of each other's teaching, and evaluate peers' practice. They used Japanese Lesson

Study as the catalyst and reported that building trust and sharing practice was central to the longevity of the project. The team affiliated with local university-based math educators as consultants, but led the work from within their site-based team.

Another example of a discipline-centered community of practice created by and for teachers comes from my neighborhood middle school music teacher. Ken is an early years' public school teacher, but a long-time professional who specializes in ethnic music performance. "As a teacher, I have found tremendous importance in collaboration with other teachers and performers. The relationships have confirmed that professional development happens only through meaningful connections with other educators and professionals in the music arena. One way I continue this growth is through the ensemble of my music colleagues in our school district 'big band.' I learn a lot from performing with my colleagues, as well as from our collaborative student performances that we organize every year."

In both situations, teachers sought professional support outside the district, behaved as both learners and teachers, and were voluntary participants in groups they identified or created. Professional respect, disciplinary knowledge, and personal relationships were important elements driving participation and satisfaction.

Another high school teacher has led a team to establish small academies in a large high school where many of the students come from families who have no experience with college. As a "first-generation college-educated Chicana," Delia recognized the lack of cultural capital in students' families. "Teachers see students every day, therefore we can have a tremendous impact on students' perceptions and the support they receive." She notes how few counselors there are and the critical role teachers play in establishing a college-going culture: "Currently, the existing comprehensive high school model hasn't given students an adequate infrastructure to increase the numbers of students of color going on to college. For this reason, we must consider other means in creating a college-going culture."

Delia works as a leader of one academy and collaborates with colleagues who are leading other academies. They formed a leadership team that collectively brings resources into the high school and takes the students into the community and neighboring universities. Teachers at this school build bridges for students to cross, spanning the chasm between inadequate public secondary schools and higher education. Delia describes her commitment to outreach and collaboration with higher education, recalling: "For the past three years, I have been part of a collaborative effort between the Career Academy Support Network in the state University Graduate School of Education, the Center on Educational Partnerships, and the System Office." These partnerships make a difference for students, particularly when teachers are the mediators of those services. School leadership also leads to districtwide leadership actions. What happens at one school will affect the workings of other schools around them, either by providing a useful model to follow or by shaming them into action.

Teachers who work in communities in transition are often drawn into community leadership roles as consultants and translators. Teachers know the families and the stories of the community members' experience in that neighborhood and beyond it. Carlos, a mid-career teacher and parent, described his community advocacy with a school that was closing. He met with families, translated policies and planning documents, outlined enrollment options for each student, and met with families several times to ensure they had the information they needed to respond to the disruption in their lives and in the children's schooling.

Finding and Using Research

Teachers conduct independent research on methods and content, often using the Internet to find resources. The next examples are excerpted from the gatekeepers activity described in

Chapter Two. Nate, a high school English department chair, led a curriculum revision effort at his school by emphasizing cross-cultural readings and activities. He described the rich diversity of races and languages portrayed in the hip hop tune "Harlem Renaissance" and noted the disparity between student ethnicity and teacher ethnicity on the national level: "In spite of broad diversity among students, the majority of teachers (who often have different ethnic backgrounds from their student constituents) are trained in methodologies that fail to address the complexity of diversity as it now exists in the United States. The Civil Rights Project, currently located on the UCLA campus, examines this topic in *Are Teachers Prepared for Racially Changing Schools?*[5] Organizations have curriculum that responds to the need for more culture awareness. However, none of those examined take U.S. secondary educational needs to its next logical evolutionary step."

Nate then used the Civil Rights Project web site (http:// civilrightsproject.ucla.edu) and other sources to identify novels, curriculum units, and other information for his colleagues to use in their instruction. His role as curriculum development leader grew from personal interest, department leadership experience, his awareness of the need, and research on the topic. His other role as department chair and his commitment to effecting change for students positioned him to develop and implement a culturally responsive curriculum.

A literacy coach in a large urban district with a high percentage of second-language speakers, Nora turned to a regional educational research nonprofit agency for resources on English language assessments for elementary students: "WestEd developed a map that identifies English language development standards and demonstrates the need for students to acquire those skills to achieve proficiency in reading and language arts. Teacher planning now revolves around identifying and using standards. Textbooks and pacing guides in science, social studies, and reading do not drive instruction—the standards do."

Nora used the research lab's materials as a foundation, working closely with school-level teams piloting different approaches to assessment that would be more useful to teachers than the prescribed materials that accompany textbooks: "Proficiency-level teams (K–2 and 3–5) will create a pacing guide during the first three weeks of school based on classroom assessments and turn that guide in to the instructional leadership team and principal to demonstrate that all standards are being met through the instructional year. Depending on student proficiency level, pacing guides will vary."

This coach now works with district-level leaders to establish more flexible assessment procedures in other schools. The research-based assessment protocols that she and her colleagues designed at one site are now informing assessment practice across the district.

In the final example, one person's vision for school-based diversity training evolved into an international teacher-led program. Seeking Educational Equity and Diversity (SEED) is an organization founded by Peggy McIntosh. Deshmukh Towery and colleagues noted McIntosh's vision of a "reflective summer week for teachers to learn from and with each other and then to convene groups in their own schools to learn from and with each other."[6] Teachers came from various regions to participate: "SEED seminars . . . are long-term interventions that help teachers to make their own schools places where all students know they belong, are valued, and can learn." The rich and diverse life experiences of teachers, skillfully facilitated, are the text and focus of this work.

Community Partnerships

Recall the discussion in Chapter Two about teachers acting "in loco parentis," in the place of parents. Interactions with students take place primarily in the classroom and at the school, but leadership actions are informed by and connected to families from the neighborhood. "Co-parenting," or bringing a parent's perspective to teaching children, has downsides. I have worked at schools in high-income and low-income communities, in the most urban and most rural corners of the country. I observe a continuum of power where parents can and do exert pressure on school staffs and district leaders. All parents should advocate for their children's welfare. Many parent concerns are justified, but parents sometimes treat teachers as another member of their staff, bringing requests or demands that their child receive different or better services. Some parents have a consumer mentality, comparing schools in their locale with data generated from standardized test scores and racial demographics before buying a house. Parents with little cultural capital fall at the other end of the spectrum, especially if they are newcomers to the country and have little or no English or economic means. In either case, the "community" with which teachers interact is primarily families, and they are teachers' primary partners.

Bringing the Community into the Classroom

Schools are residents of communities. The building is in a neighborhood, and creative teachers use the community as an extended classroom. Community members may have expertise in content areas, parents of students may volunteer in classrooms, and local businesses may donate time, money, or other kinds of support. In wealthier communities, parents write checks to support programs and people. In moderate-income or poor communities, keeping the local public school solvent is everyone's business. In many communities, the school is a place where neighbors with school-aged children see each other on a regular basis. Some neighbors who don't have children attending school come for potlucks, fundraisers, seasonal fairs, and volunteer on a Saturday morning to spruce up the grounds. Parents of students do all these things, plus attend back-to-school nights and parent conferences and chaperone field trips. Local merchants put school event posters in their windows and contribute funds to school improvement projects. When teachers are also neighbors, relationships are built outside of the school. Teachers are sometimes locals and know the community from the ground up. Others may drive in from other places, but attend political actions and shop at the neighborhood grocery store.

Nina is an art teacher in one of the poorest neighborhoods in a large urban center. Her school has benefited from community partnerships with government, nonprofit organizations, parent groups, and neighborhood redevelopment groups, among others. The neighbors still play an important role in providing energy and resources for the school: "Two neighborhood residents and artists approached me at school and asked to be involved in the art program on campus. They applied for a small grant from the city to do a public beautification project with neighborhood youth. Their goal was to design and create a decorative steel gate enameled in beautiful colors that pedestrians could walk through to enter or leave campus. With the small grant, we were able to purchase tools and materials for the enameling process that were intended to stay with the class for future use."

Neighbors and parents are generally advocates for teachers and their neighborhood school, if not always for public education more generally. During a one-day walkout recently, local teachers garnered tremendous parent support, and parents stood with teachers on the picket line. Teachers' long-term relationships with families and career-long commitment to our troubled urban district earned them appreciation and respect in the face of budget cuts.

Facilitating Cross-Cultural Conversations

In bilingual, bicultural, and multiethnic communities, teachers with ethnic backgrounds similar to students and families are indispensable leaders. These teachers offer parents and their children a critical lifeline to mainstream schooling in their new home. Teresa, a mid-career bilingual specialist at her school, states:

> My life experience of coming to the United States to live and learning a second language has helped me serve as an excellent translator at school for Spanish-speaking parents. With my good interpersonal skills, I am able to help parents relax and feel safe enough to make decisions about their child's education. Families know me and understand that they can depend upon my translation in important meetings, such as Student Study Team meetings, where many support staff and the principal are in attendance. Since the district is often unable to provide translators for every conference or meeting, my services are indeed an asset at my school.

The motivation to advocate for marginalized families often comes from teachers who share similar experiences, as Teresa described earlier. More established immigrants and middle-class bilingual teachers also recognize the need to literally speak on behalf of their students. Following are more examples of culturally competent teachers advocating for parents. In the next case, Adelle, an experienced member of her elementary school staff, observes some of her colleagues denigrating students for speaking their home language at school: "I witnessed incidents of discrimination and assumptions by two educators verbally telling students to not speak in their home language, but in English. They criticized the parents for too much school involvement, even through that involvement fostered their children's positive social interactions with other children of the school."

I note Adelle's use of "verbally telling." The phrase is not redundant, but rather a reflection that students are also "told" their languages and cultures are not acceptable through body language, exclusion from opportunity, or more explicit acts of discrimination. In the next excerpt, a senior teacher at a school targeted for closure talked directly with families and conducted his own inquiry to make recommendations to district leadership: "Through the use of parent survey-interviews, I discovered their concerns and apprehensions about having to move their children from their community school and what support they needed in the transition of their children into new schools. The web-based research I have completed supports the idea that schools, teachers, parents, and districts must have in place well-thought-out plans and procedures for parents' and students' transition into new school communities."

Carlos was dismayed by the disruption that the school closure created in the community. He responded to the situation by educating himself, families, and district leadership about more effective ways to support families through a painful transition.

Because teachers work directly with students every day, they have partnerships in place with families. Rich local knowledge can be a powerful resource, yet teachers often feel as powerless as their clients when they confront the bureaucracy. When individual events become a pattern, however, many teachers will take action in settings beyond the school. As she stated at the beginning of this chapter, Fran felt compelled by the degree of need to come out of her classroom to advocate for her students and their families. Families with fewer resources are more dependent on educators who understand their circumstances. In this excerpt, Edward, a mid-career middle school teacher, explains the changing demographic in his neighborhood school and the effect on the school staff's capacity to educate: "I can say that over the past seven years, we've seen an influx of new move-ins and more two-working-parent families than ever. Our school used to have an abundance of support of all kinds, but that has somewhat dwindled. We now have to be much more self-reliant. The infrastructure of our school as we used to know it is rapidly disappearing, and so it is much more on our backs to provide for the needs of our students."

Edward's comment reminds us that just as neighborhoods diversify, so do schools. Teachers may work for a school district, but their community, with its assets and concerns, is very local.

The examples of my colleagues' leadership demonstrate the importance of "boundary spanning"—the ability to work across classrooms, grade levels and departments, school sites, and with district and other agency representatives. The nature of classroom teaching may seem cloistered, and connections from the classroom to the district and other agencies are not always obvious. The complex requirements of managing relationships and resources are daunting. There are days when teachers need to close their doors and focus on one group for one learning event. On most days for most teachers, however, reaching out for support and consultation is a matter of professional survival for them and a matter of academic and social survival for their students.

Teacher expertise is local and organizational: teachers know about school board elections, district policy changes, pending school closures, and calendar revisions that affect students and families in the district. In the best case, communities of practice are extended to include community members to serve their needs. As Lambert tells us, "leading realizes purpose."[7] Organizations may not be human, but they are peopled by humans with gifts and challenges, budget cuts and bosses. We speak about good schools and bad schools, good districts and struggling districts, good leadership and poor leadership. What we really need are productive relationships with people who work in various parts of organizations. With some humanity and a focus on the client, we can come to a meeting of minds and transform our practice. To lead in ways that enable children and young people to learn requires crossing organizational boundaries of all kinds.

At the beginning of the book, I shared my stepping stones, or turning points, on my journey as a teacher. Most of our stepping stones involve individuals or groups who provided support, encouragement, resources, or other forms of guidance. As you consider your own journey and reach out to other individuals, teams, professional development groups, and agencies, you will find support and resources to guide your own growth and development. You may notice patterns of engagement with certain types of agencies or organizations, and you may feel more (or less) successful making connections and building relationships with other professionals. Seek to strengthen effective partnerships and add new strands to your network.

Professionals benefit directly from gaining support as well as becoming a resource for others. Knowledge creation is reciprocal, and, like the proverbial giving of love, we gain through the act of sharing our expertise. The amount of knowledge about teaching and learning is not limited, though sometimes we behave as if it were! Share what you know, and your gifts will return tenfold. The communities of practice of which we are members make the work of leading in schools possible.

An Afterword About Partnerships and Schools

I have been conscripted into partnerships, I have initiated partnerships, and I have mediated partnerships. I have worked as a school change coach for a very good nonprofit organization that supports teachers, and I currently sit on the board of another. As with any organizational process, school partnerships vary in purpose (vision), quality, personnel, politics, and reputation. As with any offering of support, the resources associated with partnerships come with strings attached. I believe that most schools can be improved by the presence of respectful, focused, purposeful relationships, and relationships with outside agencies are no exception.

In the current climate of No Child Left Behind and Race to the Top, many teachers have experienced partners as "Big Brother agency types" sent from on high (or the county office of education or state capital) to enact policy or supervise the reorganization of "failing" schools. With good reason, these individuals or teams are suspect and unwelcome. Keep an open mind anyway, and remember that all of us work within organizations that provide opportunities and challenges. Within every organization are competent educators who can work side by side with you to transform your classroom, school site, and district. The relationships you establish within these partnerships will vary in quality, but most will serve your students and your school. Remember that those partners and agencies are also the beneficiaries of your expertise. Partnerships are symbiotic, and both partners should leave with more than they had when they arrived.

Considerations About Partnering as Leading

- Work where you are, while reaching beyond that place to build and share your expertise.
- Let your student advocacy efforts guide your partnership choices.
- Partner more formally with parents and parent-led groups to benefit all students.
- Recognize and acknowledge peers in your midst who have expertise. Don't stand passively by while district leaders send outside experts into your school.
- Partner with individuals from outside schools who have influenced your thinking about teaching and learning.
- Seek support in the most obvious and the least likely places. Be vigilant about mandated reformers in your midst, but don't let skepticism or ego prevent you from using their expertise.
- Learn about the actions of nonprofit and other agencies by talking with clients and representatives, rather than judging them by hearsay.
- Be proactive to gain the most benefit from partnerships.
- Work internally with school-based leadership groups to take advantage of what partners offer, and actively manage any aspects of partnerships that are problematic.
- Consider your school a citizen of the community.

✑ INQUIRY SIX ✑
Transforming School Leadership Through Partnerships with Agencies

Seeking partners may not be a familiar task for you. You will encounter some false starts and missed connections, but don't lose sight of your goals! Remember that you and your students are part of a larger world of learning and that one partner can change your professional life and your students' opportunities to learn. To get started, identify one or more agencies or organizations that could provide resources for you and your students. Ask colleagues and neighbors, attend a conference, read the newspaper or neighborhood bulletin board, or search the Internet. The purpose of your engagement with an agency is to do the following:

1. Develop or extend professional community contacts outside of your school

2. Create or further develop your community of practice in a discipline or a general area of school reform

3. Gain broader perspectives on the value of your own work and connect to the work of others

4. Become systematic in your outreach and cross-agency strategizing

5. Show colleagues and students other avenues for their learning

In addition to those listed in the Resource sections in previous chapters, there are many more discipline-specific professional organizations. Try the following or search further.

Discipline-Specific Organizations

The History Project
http://historyproject.ucdavis.edu

National Writing Project (NWP)

www.nwp.org

National Council for the Social Studies

www.socialstudies.org

National Council of Teachers of English

www.ncte.org

National Council of Teachers of Mathematics

www.nctm.org

Science Educational Organizations

www.ncsu.edu/sciencejunction/terminal/imse/highres/2/
  horganizations.htm

Arts Education Partnership (AEP)

www.aep-arts.org

National Association for Music Education (MENC)

www.menc.org

Curriculum Connections Advanced Organizer

Topic: _____

Timeline: _____

Assessment: _____

Identify a future unit of study for your students—generally one that fits into your school's grading period, such as four weeks, six weeks, or twelve weeks long. Give yourself at least a month of lead time to prepare the unit before you plan to teach it.

1. Set up files and folders, both paper and electronic, for your unit of study.
2. Document your big ideas using your state standards.
3. Conduct online and library research to identify project-based curriculum or other innovative curriculum strategies in that field.
4. Find a person or group in your region interested in the same topic.
5. Attend a workshop, conference, or event about your topic.
6. Convene with others, whether in person or electronically, to give and offer consultation and encouragement!

Share Your Expertise

Identify a parent or community group with whom you can share your expertise. The section on gatekeepers in Chapter Two is one example. Colleagues used the Civil Rights Project's web site to research school- or education-based civil rights cases, chose a concern appropriate for their community, and make a plan to educate that audience about their rights.

Resources

Professional Education Associations.
www.unm.edu/~jka/sts/proforg.html#proflinks

Dr. Jan Armstrong created this collection of links to the web sites of many educational organizations. Most of the titles are self-explanatory, but users will need some time to open and peruse the many sites offered.

Coalition of Essential Schools (CES).
www.essentialschools.org

CES is nonprofit organization that grew out of the modern progressive education movement. CES is a network of affiliated agencies and partner schools that promotes personalized, relevant learning experiences for students through the use of ten common principles. Another focus of CES is the development of school-based study groups called "critical friends groups."

Center for Research on Education, Diversity, and Excellence (CREDE).
http://crede.berkeley.edu

This research center is housed in the Graduate School of Education at UC Berkeley and provides research, online professional development, and other resources for educators reaching across boundaries that limit student potential to succeed in school. The CREDE Five Standards for Effective Pedagogy can serve as guidelines for developing culturally responsive curriculum.

National Association for Multicultural Education (NAME).
http://nameorg.org

This organization grew out of the Association of Teacher Educators and provides information, networking, curriculum, research, and advocacy for all levels of educators seeking to diversify mainstream education. This all-volunteer organization publishes materials and research about improving the educational experiences of students and teachers of color from all levels of education.

Roots and Shoots (Jane Goodall Institute).
www.rootsandshoots.org

Founded by Dr. Jane Goodall, this international organization is leading the development of environmental
education for all ages. Through local community-based
activism, young people are taking action where they are
to address the challenges of environmental degradation.
Service learning projects offer teachers material for integrated, project-based curriculum and assessment.

Notes

The epigraph to this chapter is drawn from a quotation in B. Moyers,
A World of Ideas (New York: Doubleday, 1989).

1. B. M. Bass and R. Bass, *The Bass Handbook of Leadership: Theory,
   Research, and Managerial Applications* (New York: Simon & Schuster,
   2008).
2. P. Senge, *The Fifth Discipline: The Art and Practice of the Learning
   Organization* (New York: Currency, 1990; quotation from p. 3).
3. M. Fullen, *The New Meaning of Educational Change*, 4th ed. (New
   York: Teachers College Press, 2007); L. Lambert, M. Collay, K. Kent,
   A. Richert, and M. Dietz, *Who Will Save Our Schools? Teachers as
   Constructivist Leaders* (Thousand Oaks, Calif.: Corwin Press, 1996);
   Senge, *The Fifth Discipline*, 1990; T. Wagner and R. Kegan, *Change
   Leadership: A Practical Guide to Transforming Our Schools* (San Francisco:
   Jossey-Bass, 2006).
4. L. Lambert, "Leadership Redefined: An Evocative Context for Teacher
   Leadership," *School Leadership and Management* 23(4) (2003): 421–430
   (quotation from p. 426).
5. E. Frankenberg and G. Siegel-Hawley, *Are Teachers Prepared for Racially
   Changing Schools? Teachers Describe Their Preparation, Resources, and
   Practices for Racially Diverse Schools* (Los Angeles: Civil Rights Project,
   2008).
6. I. Deshmukh Towery, R. Oliveri, and C. L. Gidney, *Peer-Led Professional
   Development for Equity and Diversity: A Report for Teachers and
   Administrators Based on Findings from the SEED Project* (Cambridge, Mass.:
   Schott Foundation for Public Education, 2007; quotation from p. 2).
7. Lambert, "Leadership Redefined," 2003, pp. 424–425.

INDEX